HEART
of the
Marriage

Biblical quotations, unless otherwise, are taken from the Holy Bible: King James Version®. Copyright © 1984, 1977, The Amplified Bible, Copyright © 1965, 1987.

The use of selected references from various versions of the Bible in this publication does not necessarily imply endorsement of the versions in their entirety.

Interior design: Charles Rivers, Dan Robinson — The Booksetter.com
Cover Design: Charles Rivers, Dan Robinson — The Booksetter.com
Printed in the USA by Jostens, Inc., Charlotte, NC

ISBN 10: 09758984-3-7
ISBN 13: 978-09758984-3-7

FILA
PUBLISHING

HEART
of the
Marriage

*How to Mend a Challenging Relationship
and Strengthen Your Family*

CHARLES RIVERS

FILA Press

To all who support the
healing of God's marriage union

Additional Marriage Support Books by Charles Rivers

How to Get the Most In Marriage
How to Become your Spouse's Best Friend
The Good Marriage Maintenance Kit

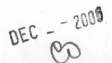

CONTENTS

Book 3 — VOLUNTEER

Book 4 — Evolve

Book 1

LEAVE
OBSERVE
VOLUNTEER
EVOLVE

*"One's unchallenged
comfort zone becomes little
more than an imprisoning wall to
the soul's ability to express
love freely."*

— Charles Rivers

*Leave
in your wake
what is self centered
in all human nature, in order to
join another soul in a shared journey called
life. Permit for yourself freely your
God given right to love
and to be loved.*

To Love One, You Must Forgive Many

S ome Christian marriages that where once red hot with passion are now less than tepid and detrimental to the emotional states of both husband and wife. When loving, committed relationships hit rock bottom, it will make you feel like planning a method of escape is the only logical solution for the pain you are causing one another. But I am here to tell you that divorce is not the answer. If you choose to walk out on your spouse, you won't be avoiding the problems of marriage. In fact, you will actually be taking those problems and concerns with you. Most people carry their own personal difficulties into their sacred marriages and subsequently depart with them intact after the divorce.

As adults, each one of us lives either for or against our own childhood upbringing. If we treasured our experiences of youth, we will more than likely seek to share them with our spouse and children within marriage. On the other hand, if our growth experiences were perceived to be more traumatic then we believed they ought to have been, then without forgiveness we will bury that awareness. But covering up pain does not make it go away; it intensifies with age if not properly healed. These unhealed wounds of the spirit are enough to cause most people to lose their spouses before losing the wounds that cause people to flee from their presence.

"A hurting
heart yields strife
in the presence of the love
it requires most."

— Charles Rivers

But what about Christian couples like yourself who are tired of letting those experiences dominate your life and ruin your happiness? What about people like you who engage in Godly self help books and counseling because you desire to heal what you know is best for your Christian life? Is it possible to resurrect the shared love that you once held close to your heart?

Yes, it is possible and if you earnestly apply what you learn here you can make it permanent in your relationship, and not just for a season. First and foremost, cancel any thought of flights of fancy towards divorce. Heading for the front door is far more painful than heading for any kind of face to face reconciliation.

Whether I'm traveling on the road or teaching locally, I find that most couples, be they Christian or secular, bring more issues and concerns with them to the marriage than they could ever generate within it. In fact, I can honestly say that I have never held a seminar or taught a marriage session where the problems were solely based in the relationship. Most problems and angers were triggered by hurts and dislikes from their childhood past reflected within their current married lives. Their fantasies of divorce were compounded by the need to escape the same pains that had dominated their early lives for many years.

> *Most complaints and*
> *concerns we have about our*
> *mates are not as much*
> *about them as they*
> *are about us.*

> *— Charles Rivers*

The roots of anger, pressure or stress originate when people's own environments or circumstances are acting out of their personal wills, and not out of God's will. Calmness can only be achieved once people surrender their will and intentions for themselves, other people and environment over to God from which they came. Therefore, as a husband, if I am angered by or dislike something my wife does, I can easily trace it back to not liking that same behavior in someone or something in my youth.

What follows are several true short stories of couples whose lives were negatively affected by past unforgiving events. In holding fast to these negative memories, each person was brought very close to losing their spouse. It is impossible to have a great marriage without God or forgiveness. We will discuss the resolution of these problems and many others later on in this book in the section entitled, "Learning How to Forgive."

Alex's Story — Alex, at times, appears to enjoy shouting down every good suggestion his wife makes as silly or without merit. He mocks her achievements as nothing more than the vanity of a spoiled rich kid. Shelly, his wife, says that she has no earthly idea where all of Alex's animosity and criticisms are coming from. Alex, when questioned about his critiques of Shelly, refuses to admit his comments are any more than innocent teasing. All of Shelly's life she has gone after her dreams with the support and backing of her parents. But lately she has begun to doubt her dreams for the future and the hopes of this marriage lasting past this year. Every since she married Alex, she has found herself scaling back her goals so that she does not overshadow his wishes for her.

Alex's Dilemma — As a boy, Alex grew up in a home where his family routinely diverted him away from his God-given talent in favor of him following in his father's chosen foot steps. When success did not materialize for Alex in the field his parents chose for him, they deemed Alex a failure. As an adult, he recalled to me in one session how he came to be attracted to Shelly. He commented that she exhibited all of the high drive and determination that he once possessed for himself. Alex said to me, "*Mr. Rivers, Shelly was one girl that used to stand up for herself no matter what people thought of her. But lately it seems that she has withdrawn from that passionate drive she once had. I'm doing everything I know possible to motivate her.*"

Alex did not realize that he was the root cause for the change in Shelly's behavior. It was nothing he had set out intentionally to do at the onset of the relationship, but it was something that materialized over time because Alex had never addressed it prior to marriage. Unfortunately, Alex had not yet forgiven his parents for a wrong he perceived they visited upon him. Now his relationship is in ruins because he responds to his wife as his parents once responded to him. His envy of Shelly's achievements doesn't have much to do with Shelly—it has to do with Shelly's parents. What appeared to be envy of her achievements grew out of a desire for a more supportive upbringing.

Nina's Story — Nina made it emphatic when she married her husband Pete that she would not tolerate adultery in any form. Although Pete has carried a strict monogamous stance for marriage since he was a little boy, Nina's fears were not allayed. Nina, wanting to play it safe all her life, has been careful to marry a man who believes in strict monogamy — yet in still she has no trust in her husband's fidelity. Over the last five years of marriage she has kept fears of infidelity close to her heart in hopes of staying sharp enough to catch her husband committing adultery. This type of behavior on Nina's behalf has destroyed every moment of closeness a loving relationship has to offer. Nina is prompt to tell Pete, her husband, she does not trust his fidelity to her any further than knowing his whereabouts. Though she considers herself a God loving Christian, she refers to all men, including Pete, as animals and unfaithful cheaters.

Nina's Dilemma — As a child, little Nina was raised in a home where her father flagrantly cheated on her mother. She has had at least seven failed relationships prior to marriage with men she knew to be unfaithful. Her fears of a committed relationship grew out of what she witnessed between her parents and have nothing to do with Pete. If Nina is unable to forgive her upbringing, she will continue to make her husband Pete pay penitence for the entire species of man.

Margaret's Story — Over the last forty years, Margaret has grown to believe that she is equal only to what she has attained by wealth or status. Not a weekend has passed that she has not made extremely high purchases on her credit cards in order to line the walls of her already crowded home. Margaret has been known to spend so many weekends at the mall that the employees at particular stores have come to associate her as a family member. With a now overly hectic work schedule to support her booming lifestyle, she finds that she has less and less time to spend with her husband and children. Her conversations with her coworkers are little more than bolstering of what she owns or will attain next. Over the last ten years, Margaret's household has grown rich in material goods but impoverished in love because of the lack of intimacy money can't buy.

*"For whatever is
pressed down upon us
becomes us, unless we are
willing to forgive our
transgressors."*

— Charles Rivers

Margaret's Dilemma — Margaret grew up in a time where the national economy took such a bad hit that it caused both of her parents to become unemployed. To save money for critical needs, her parents imposed severe frugality on their lives. They withdrew Margaret from a private school that she had come to love. They sold a home that had been paid off and moved to a lower income neighborhood to devote their income to a mountain of debt acquired before the downturn of the economy. Margaret remembers going to school for many years in clothes from stores that sold only seconds. In Margaret's young mind, her parents were failures because they lost everything in her eyes. The fact that her mother had another child while their finances were low only cemented this in Margaret's mind.

She recalls that her parents did all they could to keep the family strong back then, even though the finances were not. Margaret believed that she and her newborn sister dragged down the finances of the family. She thought that it would have been easy if her parents were free to pursue wealth instead of supporting children. Her parents did not recall this at all; what they remembered is that this was the best time in their lives. They recanted how this brought them back to understanding what was really important, namely family. Margaret did not receive that message, even though her parents had recovered much more than they lost only twelve years after the downturn.

Craig's Story — Craig has entered his second year of marriage terse and bitter towards his wife, Monica. He identifies every serious discussion between Monica and himself as a personal attack on his manhood. Each attempt Monica makes to find resolution in the growing rift between them is met with the silence or indifference. Monica recounts that she has heard Craig say on many occasions that she will "never be able to dominate him, so don't even try."

Craig's Dilemma — As a boy, Craig watched his mother speak to his father in a demeaning fashion on a daily basis throughout their marriage. None of Craig's extended family members knew back then why it was that Craig's father stayed with his wife. Viewing his parents locked in a loveless marriage, Craig promised himself that his marriage would never be that way. As an adult, his choice for a wife was completely the opposite of his mother's personality and demeanor. He remembers choosing to marry Monica over all of the other women he dated because she had a loving and gentle spirit.

But lately Craig has not been honoring that spirit. His deliberate rudeness to his wife extends from his erroneous belief that he will end up being bullied by his wife as his father was by his mother. Craig is now living the exact life that he had planned to avoid many years ago. The only difference is he is acting out the role of his mother instead of the position his father took. In fact, Craig unconsciously chose Monica because she would emulate his father's tolerance of bad behaviors.

Lisa's Story — Lisa's marriage to her husband, Paul, has been teetering off and on the brink of divorce for the last six months of a two year marriage. In the beginning months of their new marriage romance between them had been wonderfully charming. But now that they have been married for only a short time, Lisa has begun to recoil from Paul's physical touch. Lisa explained to me that she does not mean to hurt Paul's feelings but that she does not desire this type of intimacy with him or anyone else right now. Lately even Paul's gazes of admiration are becoming little more than painful stings of lust in Lisa's eye.

Lisa's Dilemma — As a child, little Lisa was repeatedly molested by her father in what should have been the safest place on earth, namely her own home. Her perception of sex since that time has been tainted as nothing more than a filthy way men receive gratification. Sometimes the unforgiving pains of childhood hurt as many as five generations that follow the initial trauma. Childhood pains can affect your spouse just as much as they do you, for in marriage not only do you share names but pains, pleasures and past experiences.

To add insult to injury, as a little girl, Lisa had no comforting arms to fall into. She recounts with animosity how her own mother chose not to believe what was going on in the home. Determined not to be hurt anymore, Lisa chose Paul because he appeared to be a non-threatening caring man that could help her through her intimacy issues. But Paul can never succeed at helping Lisa as long as she keeps her past a secret from him.

Lisa, like many other people, became acutely aware of the pains she hides if they are reflected by other people in everyday life. In her case, the advances of her husband mirrored the molesting advances of her parent. In fact, reflecting back becomes very dangerous because we end up focusing only on the hurt in the midst of great pleasure all around us each day. This sense of unresolved pain blinds our vision where our pre-hurt memories once gave us sight. This is why I adamantly tell all couples I get the chance to influence to turn your hurts and pains over to God. Because only God and the power of forgiveness allows us to lift the thin veil of blindness that has been blocking our sight to joy.

In John 9:25 we witness as the once blind man stands before the Pharisees virtually on trial for being cured on the Sabbath. He is questioned on the ethics of whether Jesus was a sinner due to the fact that he cured him on this holiest of days. His response to their accusations of blasphemy was simple when he said, "*I do not know whether this man is a sinner or what you say of him, but one thing I do know, I was blind but now I see!*"

I believe this healing was symbolic of what Jesus can do for all persons who have gone through pains or tragedy and have become blinded to what is the best in them and their relationships with their fellow human beings. For this man had not done any sin that would call down the punishment of blindness. But in his healing of blindness he experiences the same release from bondage that anyone of us would from past injuries.

The Greatest Journey Begins

In this the first book entitled leave we are going to learn how to **leave** what was self centered in our nature behind in order to grow with the one we have pledged our marriage vows to. All growth in life starts with a process of surrendering what we believed to be our personal truths, not God's. So if your marriage has become stagnant you will have to leave the level you have become accustomed to in order to experience the next highest love.

*"For one does not mature
primarily based upon who
they are, but who they
are not thus far."*

— *Charles Rivers*

When Loss Is Gain

From the time of Adam and Eve to our present time, God has always called a person, a couple or a people to leave either who they are or where they are in order to make them great. The path to growth has always been one that is preceded by leaving your old self behind. In the eyes of God, your marriage is no different. Examine for yourself the biblical principle of those who left the old self behind to begin anew. When God calls upon us to leave, it will be for one of three things.

It might be for our health, as when he sent the angels in Genesis 12:1-3 to tell Abraham to *leave Sodom* before he destroyed the town.

It might be for our personal growth, as when God told all men in Genesis 2:24 to *leave their fathers and mothers behind* and cleave to their spouse. But the one command to leave that most people prefer is the last: when the Lord tells us to leave for the sake of gaining wealth, as when he told Moses in Genesis 31:12-14 to leave Egypt and go to possess a land flowing with milk and honey that he will give them. Now if God the Father tells you to leave for all three reasons you may count yourself as blessed. But if he allows you to marry someone before leaving the person you are behind you should count yourself as doubly blessed. For in doing this God is sending someone on the journey with you to comfort and keep you in times of plenty and in times of want.

"Marriage, is
not about control; in
fact it is the opposite of control.
It exists on the realm of mysteries and
like a mystery only best when carefully
unfolded. Where as a controlled
environment becomes insistent
upon a very narrow
fixed outcome."

— *Bridget Rivers*

Conflict Occurs Where
Controlling Behaviors Persist

On a gorgeous autumn afternoon I was scheduled to receive a Christian couple who were at the brink of divorce with little faith left in the institution of marriage. My wife and constant companion, Bridget, met this young couple at the headquarters of our counseling center, *Falling In Love Again*. Bridget, as usual, saw to it that they were received as graciously as possible. Within a short time I joined them in the conference room, where we had developed a warm, loving environment for centering the attitudes of stressed out couples. This day would not be business as usual, for this couple would become my greatest inadvertent teachers of strife resolution in marriage.

I sat mesmerized in that conference room at the sight of a devout Christian couple cynically tearing each other apart. Husband and wife had a pad and pen with which they would jot down retaliatory comments to be levied against one another's accusations. This was so that they could address each issue defensively and with strength while the other person ceased to speak for just a moment. I noted in my comments log how, with the mastery of a tenured scholar, they easily quoted biblical verses in support of their past offenses in opposition to one another. On this day God and the bible would sit in defense of their misdeeds more than this couple would be willing to.

Not only could husband and wife successfully quote the passages and paragraphs of their bible but probably the line item with page number. For many people this would be a difficult feat at best, but not for the Smiths, for they were raised in church. In fact, Tim's father was a minister his entire adult life until the day he died a few years earlier. What each spouse failed to understand was that they were doing little more than what I refer to as "twist quoting" the bible. For in no way does the bible justify bad behavior or strife between husband and wife.

One verse in particular that Mr. Smith continually chose to twist quote in his favor was the same verse most Christian men lean upon when they are being denied sexual relations by their wives.

Mr. Smith quoted to his wife, in my presence, the bible verse that states, *"For the wife's body is not her own but the husband's."* In this belief, regardless of how tattered their relationship was, everything would magically heal itself if she would just go to bed with him. Sure they would despise one another, but his sexual desires would be satisfied along with his need for love. Their relationship had run its course for eleven years this way and would not make it one more day under these conditions.

"It is incumbent
upon men to appreciate
that a woman can no more yield
her body in anger to sex, then a man
would friendship to one who
opposes him."

— *Charles Rivers*

I knew for a fact that Mrs. Smith had her own personal issues, but at least she was in pursuit of true love. But the true love she sought was from her father through other men, which had resulted only in sexual love. By the time we met, Mrs. Smith confessed to me that she was tired of men altogether. She thought maybe if she could just settle for the divorce everything would be fine over time. Too long, in her estimation, had she held out hope for her husband to show her true love. With each passing day, the more her husband refused to show real love the angrier she grew. There were several times in their private home when she would get so angry with herself that she would physically lash out at her husband. But actually, she was really wishing to lash out at her father.

The Smiths were a couple seriously out of the will of God and therefore blinded to his power to heal their marriage. The husband misjudged his wife as merely a piece of sexual property given to him by God. This alienated the husband from his own humanity by his misinterpretation of the Father's word. In coming to know Mr. Smith over some period of time, I would come to understand that his disrespect for her grew from his disillusionment with his mother.

Mr. Smith was silently angry at his mother for her resistance to his father when he was a minister. For all of the work his father did in the church, he could never convert a resistant wife. Mr. Smith's mother had always tried to lead the family contrary to every decision the father made. Even beyond Mr. Smith's father's death, the mother continued to interfere in the lives of her adult children. As an adult, Mr. Smith somehow reasoned it was his job to browbeat and convert his wife because his father failed to effect change in his spouse.

Mrs. Smith had her own inner turmoil to deal with that had lasted since her troubled youth. She still harbored hatred in her heart for her father, who had molested her as a little child. Her disdain for her husband was similar to many cases where the husband, in the mind of the wife, takes up where the father left off.

The Smith's difficulty was not that they couldn't achieve high marks at any Christian academy for accuracy of the bible's books. Their deficit was in they had no love for one another and not a lot of respect for themselves long before they ever came to pay me visit. To have the ability to discern the bible truthfully and activate its power in your everyday life, you must have love. The Apostle Paul wrote to the church of Corinth that, *"If anyone imagines that he has come to know and understand much [of divine things, without love,] he does not perceive and recognize and understand as strongly and clearly, nor has he become as intimately acquainted with anything as he ought or as is necessary."* 1 Corinthians 8:2

"Sweetheart,
the bible is written to
where it would confound
any sinner."

— Joyce Drumming

Would Having More Sex or Attaining More Wealth Improve Your Marriage?

Nothing could be further from the truth. Even if every therapist in the world took a vote and agreed upon it. Most adults have had sex numerous times prior to marriage. Within a marriage of some ten years or more, a couple may have had sex several thousand times. One more sexual moment would not add an ounce of love to a person's life. Therefore having sex with your spouse or anyone else could never make you sexually satisfied. The sense of satisfaction with who you are must come from within because sexual love or erotic love is more of a state of mind then it is a true love. Concerning money, you could follow the wages of a medium income family from the time they marry until the time of death and you may learn something that most people never consider: together a married couple could collectively make several millions of dollars over their lifetime. Even though many people may not have much to show for it down the road, earning one more dollar would not draw any more love to their relationship because money in and of itself will not buy you inward fulfillment. The Lord our heavenly Father has designed a way for couples to live life and enjoy love to its fullest since the time of Adam and Eve. Yet very few couples tap into the true love nature that all marriages possess. Love is our only power to call down God's unmerited blessings and favor; likewise it is that same power that can draw redemption to our troubled relationships.

Why Traditional Counseling Fails

Traditional secular counseling fails couples because it originates from the reasoning's of man's mind minus the will of God. Traditional secular counseling seeks to implant theories and solutions into the consciousness of the human psyche. God's word, on the other hand, is infallible and in its purpose seeks only to pull clarification out of man's soul in order to activate his consciousness. Only God the Father knows the heart of man, which is why he implanted solutions to the troubles that plague us in advance of birth on an individual case by case basis.

The non-Christian counselor who does not acknowledge God has made themselves the final approving authority on the message he/she seeks to give you. If he/she does not draw their authority from God to heal your relationships, where do they get it? If it comes from self or psychiatry alone, then you are looking at the highest approving authority in your life. For the bible tells us in Proverbs 6:1, "The plans of the mind and orderly thinking belong to man, but from the lord comes the [wise] answer of the tongue. All the ways of a man are pure in his own eyes but the lord weighs the spirit."

"What weight can any counsel
apply to the act of forgiveness
if it does not originate from
the mouth of God?"

— *Charles Rivers*

But for true marriages the most priceless gift the Creator can bestow upon us is the gift of discernment. The spirit of relationship discernment should be the most prized in the Christian home over secular advice. For without these gifts all else between the Creator and the created become lost in translation. The bible in the hands of the non-discernable is nothing more than a Shakespearean novel to be read cover to cover. In fact, we are cautioned about trying to understand the spirit of God through the natural man verses the spiritual man.

In 1st Corinthians 2:14 Paul tells us, *"But the natural, nonspiritual man does not accept or welcome or admit into his heart the gifts and teachings and revelations of the Spirit of God, for they are folly to him; and he is incapable of knowing them because they are spiritually discerned and estimated and appreciated."*

The Myth of Compatibility

Many studies have been done in the scientific communities that suggest that compatibility is best for marriage longevity. This hoax has been the worst fraud ever perpetrated against the institution of marriage since its inception. For if compatibility was the panacea of all marriage ills, as it is claimed to be, then why is the institution of marriage over eight thousand years old? The very nature of God's creation of man and woman dispels this belief. Because out of all of the Father's natural wonders, the human was the only one developed with a critically disagreeable mind. Therefore it would take a huge stretch of the imagination for two free thinking persons to always agree on every decision.

When God saw that Adam was alone in the Garden of Eden he decided that he would make him a helpmate. Now here is where things get tricky for the scientific community. God had a choice to create a clone-like male as Adam for a friend, but he did not. Instead he created Eve, who was not only the complete opposite of Adam, but so were her thoughts, wishes and dreams. To make Eve completely compatible with Adam, you would have to either destroy her free will or make her brain respond as an extension of Adam's thoughts.

This was not to be so in God's kingdom, for even in the children that are born to man, each one is representative of their own hopes, dreams and aspirations. In all of God's creations, natural love combined with free will becomes the glue that holds the relationship together. The Father left intact the human marriage with the same free will that allowed the apple to be drawn from the tree of good and evil. He left it up to husband and wife to join and come to a consensus despite their backgrounds or income.

This is important information for couples to know who wish no evil to ever befall their relationship. God the Father took the same risk in the Garden of Eden that any husband or wife does in placing their trust in the person they choose to marry. That risk being that your greatest love may be pulled away from you by their own unfettered free will. If he believed in compatibility he would have made our brains extensions of his control, thereby killing the concept of free will.

In 1st Corinthians 13:5 The Apostle Paul further dispels this myth when he writes, *"Love (God's love in us) does not insist on its own rights or its own way, for it is not self seeking."*

Further proof of the Creator's incompatibility theory is that no one has ever been born with the exact facial features or fingerprints of another. You could even have two twins grow up in the same home their entire lives and end up as they started, completely incompatible. The scientific community has natural love wrong if they persist in reducing it to methodical formulas. In life, we put more consideration into finding an employee for a new job position than in choosing a spouse.

Why? Because the employer seeks an employee who is compatible with his wishes and goals. The employer wants an employee who will take orders at any time, day or night, without complaint. This type of working relationship for money is the opposite of free will and marriage. Compatibility is a flawed science for love, for it chooses love from the thoughts of the mind, while true love (Gods love), chooses to love from the heart, which is blind to all formulas of the mind.

What Drives Christians to Secular Counselors and Divorce?

The very same unhealed areas that motivate secular couples to part one another's company drive Christians to secular counselors and divorce. Namely, a lack of knowledge concerning Godly relationships coupled with a strong fear of what we cannot control within the marriage. But here are just two reasons why no married Christian should seek to haphazardly divorce without seeking resolution. Primarily because God our heavenly father will not be pleased. You will find very few stated periods in the bible where God himself is moved to use the word hate. But In Malachi 2:16 God tells us clearly, "*For the Lord the God of Israel, says: I hate divorce and marital separation, and him who covers his garment (his wife) with violence.*"

Secondly, when we walk away and get a divorce from our spouse in situations that could have been worked through, we repeat the mocking patterns of Lucifer, Cane and Jonah. These chosen representatives of the Father in effect turned their backs on God for the sake of selfish motives. In the case of Lucifer, he could not stand to be under God's authority, so he plotted a rebellion to take over God's kingdom. In his overestimation of self worth, the only kingdom he came to inherit was the kingdom of hell.

In the case of Cain, he could not stand to be upstaged by his brother Abel in the eyes of God. So not only did he kill his brother for selfish reasons but he hid his body. Because of this, Cain not only lost his inheritance of that same land but he was cast out into an unknown world. In Jonah's case he could not stand to climb to God's level of forgiveness for the Ninevites, who he despised very much for their past indiscretions.

So Jonah lowered his own expectations of being proud to serve the Lord and ultimately fled God's purpose for selfish reasons. For this reason God allowed him to be cast into the mouth of the whale until he was ready to rise to the level of what he knew to be right. Each story represents how the character failed to submit humble service unto the Lord. Today we are faced with this same dilemma in marriage because couples refuse to submit humble service unto one another.

We Create More Hurt Than We Avoid by Playing Things Safely

A lack of knowledge as a destruction tool in relationships is understandable, but what activates fear from love? Pain activates fear, past pains of physical, mental or emotionally unhealed areas. For example, if a friend and I wanted to take my parents' car for a joy ride without permission. During our lesson in stealing, we got into a near-fatal car accident — then something mysterious took place. By facing our mortality, we have become cautious to the experience of driving altogether. Many years later, long after the initial traumatic experience has passed, we remain in a state of avoidance when we get behind the wheel.

In getting behind the wheel, we become mentally paralyzed by memories triggered from our past. These closely held fears destroy what otherwise would have been a pleasant driving experience. If we are to grow to enjoy driving once again, we must break free from this feeling of long ago experiences.

"One can never
truly experience the
abundant fruits of love whose
heart remains guarded by
past hurts and fears."

— Charles Rivers

Recently at a grocery store, while discussing the union of marriage with a friend of mine, I was abruptly interrupted by a patron who was standing close behind. This woman, over hearing what I do to help couples, quickly exclaimed, "Oh I'm never going to get married!" Now I normally understand that when I receive comments similar to this that there is a painful experience in the person's past. So I retorted back to her, "Why is that, ma'am?" She rebutted with the remark, "Oh marriage ruins a good relationship." I then asked her if she was currently in a committed relationship. "Yes," she replied, "I have had a live-in boyfriend for the last seven years and we have two children together."

This honest woman had just unknowingly walked right into a lifelong lesson. I asked her honestly, "How is your live-in relationship at present?" With a changed countenance, she replied, "Not good at all!" With that little bit of knowledge I pondered this life-changing scenario. Let's say you had been married to this same man for seven years with these same two children. Along the way of this seven-year relationship, you developed a similar not-so-good relationship which caused you to divorce. What then is the difference of living with him seven years the identical way without a ring? Far too many of us are willing not to be together in marriage over technicalities like a ring and certificate. A wedding band won't change the character of a person who is good or bad — it will only enhance those character traits.

"When we allow
past injuries and pains
to guide our daily existence,
we end up going forward in
life with a rear thinking
mind set."

— Charles Rivers

To live with the opposite gender over getting married does not change the fact that you are living in a marriage situation. God originally brought Eve to Adam in the Garden of Eden without the assistance of a wedding ring or certificate of marriage. Sure times have changed and the Government of each country regulates the institution over its original monitors: the church. But remember God did not turn the marriage of Adam to Eve down because of the absence of a ring. Nor did he ask them to come back in about six thousand years after the justice of the peace was invented to get the certificate.

As humans, we fear pain that comes from objects or people that we are attracted to only after the experience. But you see, since the time of infancy, attraction to anything in life starts the educational process — if we will allow it. The boys in the car accident were originally attracted by the car. The woman who is attracted to an unknown man enters a relationship that brings problems in marriage. If we can bring ourselves beyond the pain, we can ultimately arrive at the pleasure. You will never get a good marriage without first getting your hands down dirty and deep within it.

When I receive couples who approach me with the belief that their problems are mountainous, I tell them congratulations. I congratulate them because a problem-free relationship is not really a relationship at all. Now they have something in common that is real to them. Pooling our faith in God during times of trouble or disagreements allows couples an assurance of a brighter tomorrow. We are promised in Matthew 17:20 that, *"If you have the faith like a grain of mustard seed, you can say to this mountain, Move from here to yonder place, and it will move; and nothing will be impossible to you."*

So it is within the marriage relationship that couples can merge their faith and move any mountain together. Because in life problems will befall all Godly relationship to draw the couple closer together — not pull them apart. Couples who believe in a fantasy relationship get disappointed with each real life scenario that happens upon their home, even though they are powerless to avoid it. Each problem given by the universe presents itself upon our homes on an inclining scale.

These problems start low at one end and continue to climb with ever higher intensity and sophistications until the couple jointly brings them to resolution. If the Christian couple chooses not to answer its call to resolution, it will not go away. Couples who come to me with many problems that span several years usually arrive with the belief that things will never be resolved. But I have found in working with couples for the last decade that the opposite holds true. Some of the most painful relationships turn out to be more loving and binding after resolution then they ever were before.

A healed relationship is far more interpersonal then the original one we tried to live flawlessly under. Most relationships that part before the healing process divide under angered circumstances that taint society's view of the institution of marriage. In subsequent relationships each divorcee eventually end up putting their new partner in the same old light as their spouses were made to be judged by. An angered divorced person will run them through many grueling tests at arms length to make them prove their love before reciprocating in kind. This type of behavior will only serve to invite the same pain they had sought to leave behind in the previous relationship.

Moving Beyond the Fears of Pain to the Healing Process

Before people can free themselves of the past pains that affect their current relationship they must first understand how fear damages love. Some relationships have a fear of past relationship failures. For example, your parent's relationship might have ended in divorce and divided an otherwise beautiful family. We become preoccupied with wondering whether these distressing experiences will affect our marriage now. Other couples have a fear of their present happiness fading away over time. This is the representative by a "we are so happy as a couple now; will it last?" syndrome.

Finally, most relationships that fail become possessed by the remaining fears of the future. The fear of the future predicts that we will not be able to make it until death do us part before we separate or divorce. It leaves couples to wonder if they will destroy their children's lives by becoming a divorce statistic. These fears destroy marriages at all stages because the home is being dominated by the demonic control of fear. If past fears in life threaten your home, you must excise them in order to save your relationship and your very life. Why? Because God the Father does not give us a spirit of fear. The Apostle Paul writes to Timothy, *"For God did not give us a spirit of fear, but of power and of love and of calm and well balanced mind and discipline and self control"* (2 Timothy 1:7).

Where there is fear present, love cannot coexist. Light and darkness cannot cohabitate the same space at the same time. Love comes from God, and fear from the devil. But whatever is greatest in your home will be the demise of the weaker. In 1st John 4:18 we are told, *"There is no fear in love (dread does not exist), but full-grown (complete, perfect) love turns fear out of doors and expels every trace of terror! For fear brings with it the thoughts of punishment and (so) he who is afraid has not reached the full maturity of love [Is not yet grown into loves complete perfection].*

The second element of eliminating fear in our relationships is in the attainment of knowledge (God's knowledge). God's knowledge is truth, and the bible tells us, *"that the truth will make us free."* But without the truth, the bible says, in Hosea 4:6, that, *"My people are destroyed for lack of knowledge."* Our human fears are only a state of mind, an emotion aroused by impending pain in this situation. The only lawful fear, as told to us in the bible, is in reverence for God. Beyond this we are told countless times in the bible to *fear not.* We need love and knowledge to shine the light of truth on the darkness and fear that have a grip upon our relationships.

Fear of anything in our lives will lead to that thing's ultimate ruin. Fear of what should have been a loving marriage will result in its destruction.

The Rebirth of Relational Knowledge in Your Marriage

The best example I can give you to infuse God's love in a hurry into your relationship has existed since the dawn of man. We will model this behavior throughout this book and your life to heal your closeness as a Christian couple. We will be discussing this knowledge key more in depth in book 2, entitled *Observe*.

But I must say that no matter whether I am giving a one on one marriage enrichment session with a husband and wife, mass seminars or radio addresses, I always ask this question first:

> *"Why is it that a typical friendship*
> *is capable of lasting twenty years,*
> *while a marriage is hard pressed*
> *to last barely two?"*

> — *Charles Rivers* ©1998

Now I have received varied answers to this question over the many years I have taught this course in love. But for some reason the answers usually come back to me in the form of rhetorical questions. They are what I jokingly refer to as questionable answers. I receive answers such as, "Isn't it because friends don't live together and that is why their relationship last longer then marriages?"

But the true answer to that question is the solution to all of your relationship problems as well as God's solution for the unhealed relationship. I further suggest to husbands and wives that my instruction be used to change themselves and not their spouse. Just as easily as you picked up this book and made it a tool for change in your life, so can your spouse. Why do I say this? Because it is impossible to change anyone without first getting their permission.

> *"All true change*
> *occurs from within and*
> *not from without."*

> — *Charles Rivers*

Let's see what happens when you try to force change upon a child concerning something that they are dead set against. How many of us remember sitting for long periods at mom's kitchen table because we refused to eat our vegetables? At a young age children will take a liking more to sugars than they ever will to vegetables or what is right for them. As parents, we end up looking like the bad guy as we try to induce our children to do or eat right.

But no amount of prodding or strong will on our behalf will ever make our children convert to doing something they don't want to do naturally. In fact, if you put pressure on your children beyond a certain limit, you risk hurting them or permanently setting them against ever liking what you are trying to promote in their lives. The same applies to your spouse giving you love as you believe he or she should or changing a negative behavior to a positive one.

If one spouse tries to force feed his or her opinions or views of life on the other without love, he or she risks solidifying inaction regarding that problem. It is easier to elicit a negative response from someone's behavior than it is to get positive. But to change someone from negative to positive requires your support and the hand of the Almighty. Anything less will be short-lived or something other than genuine behavior.

Don't Walk Out on Your Husband or Wife Just Yet

*"There is no challenge
in loving someone who
loves you back."*

— *Charles Rivers*

I was once asked for counsel by a man who was completely frustrated with his wife's attitude about him and their marriage. But he truly loved her and he wanted to see her happy but he did not know how long he should wait for her to come around. I told him to give her another eighteen years before he entertained any thoughts of walking out on her.

At that moment he looked at me like I was crazy. "Another eighteen years? Are you sure about that?" "Yes," I said, "give her another eighteen years at the minimum without any consideration of what happens." Then I proceeded to explain to him what that number symbolized. You see, most people grew up in the home of their mother; others may have had to live with a grandparent or relative. Even to a lesser extent, some children grew up adopted or in foster care. But during those growing years you had a parent who cared for you when you were not at your best. When you were transitioning through your rebellious or angry stage.

Those were the parents who stood by us when we did things that were detrimental to our safety and our future successes. They loved us when we were unlovable, because any parent worth their salt knows one thing: when it comes to children, there is no challenge in loving someone who loves you back. The challenge is loving your child through them hating you until they come around to becoming what was best in them. So yes, I expected him to stay with his wife the same way his mother stayed with and loved him. I am grateful to report that he is now living up to that eighteen year period of reciprocal support. I similarly expected his wife to change her behaviors and show him love in kind.

"Love has a
very short shelf life;
ensure that you give it away
before it goes bad."

— *Charles Rivers*

What Happens After the Change Occurs From Within?

Back at mother's house we may not have enjoyed those vegetables we deemed icky but somehow, over time, we grew to accept them. A decade or so later you would not have believed we were the same children who snuck those vegetables to the trash can. As adults, our taste buds changed along with our desires for diverse meals. Now we take those same vegetables we could not stand and eat them at least once per week on our own. We coat them with butter, maybe cheese; sometimes we eat them al dente. In fact, if we are feeling wild enough, we can eat them without the meal altogether. Our mothers remain shocked, wondering if these are the same children that wept instead of eating those horrible peas. Love (God's love in us) gives space for growth, time for healing and understanding to pain.

Our Problems Are Not My Fault!

Many husbands and wives attend counseling sessions with a gospel belief that they are absolved of all wrong in a shared relationship. I let couples who come to my office know that I do not believe in the blame game and I would not allow them to play it with each other either. Blame will only hold you hostage to unresolved issues. One thing is for sure: once poison, hatred or bitterness has crossed our collective doorstep, it will remain the full time job of both partners to individually and cooperatively remove it.

Even if we believe ourselves to be the blameless one, trust me when I say the experience has changed you. As a husband and father, I can catch and bring home the flu (a metaphor for bitterness) and, without knowing, easily spread it to my wife and children. But to get the house cured of the illness will require a collective effort on the parts of all of its inhabitants: including the children.

Sure, I could go out and purchase the flu medicine needed to heal myself (religious counseling), but I could never heal my family with all of the medicine I take. Nevertheless, I could bring soup (a metaphor for love), juice and cool towels to my wife and children until my family was back to wellness. Once we have regained strength as a family, we could disinfect the entire house by letting the love of God into our home to guard against future viruses. So you see, it does not matter who the perceived bad guy is when there is anger and hatred present.

> *"Hatred is like taking a*
> *poisonous pill and expecting*
> *the other person that you aim*
> *that hatred at to die."*
>
> *— Author unknown*

This title available at
www.heartofthemarriage.com

"Love endures long and is patient and kind; Love never is envious nor boils over with jealousy, is not boastful or vainglorious, does not display itself haughtily."

1 Corinthians 13:4

You Will Remove a Bounty of Dirt Before You Reach Gold

In all relationships that are unhealed, couples fuss and fight depending on where their relationship lies within them. For some people the relationship lies within the heart and for many others it exists merely in their heads. Is your relationship in your head or in your heart? A relationship that rests in your heart is a loving one. A relationship that resides in the head is of a controlling nature or a reasoning of the mind.

A relationship in the heart says: I brought you these flowers as a symbol of the love I feel for you. A relationship in the head says: I brought you these flowers because I am trying to manipulate you for something I have done or need down the road. If you are in a relationship that is not based in the heart, do not dismay for everyone has a redemptive nature that leads us back to the heart.

If you or your spouse has turned negative, a more positive nature is just a pick and a shovel away. If we are to get to the real worth or gold of a relationship, often times we will have to remove a lot of dirt, rocks and silt. If left alone, these problems creep up to choke the life's blood out of all loving relationships. If left unaddressed, we blame our spouses in place of the actual people who caused us these harms initially.

The Properties of Gold are the Same as the Attributes of Love

God's love, as inherited by man, is eternal and always has a redemptive nature. Did you know that gold is the only substance that does not oxidize or corrode? In fact, most space missions that launch satellites have wires that use gold as a conductor instead of any other element. Scientists know that the rigors of constant heat and cold wreak havoc and corrode all other alloys but gold.

This is also why the gold on the satellite, in some cases, is worth more than its technology. This is chiefly because the components of the computers will fail long before the gold turns a century old unblemished. That is why its alloy is the best representative of love. In 1st Corinthians 13:4 it states that, *"love never fails or becomes obsolete or comes to an end."* This is the strength of gold as well, why then would we settle for less in our marriage relationships then we do with our personal wealth?

End Your Search for False Gold

Many good people enter relationships by going through the same processes as a person looking for effortless gold. Most of us are content to settle for pyrite or what is known as fool's gold. Fool's gold mimics the consistency of true gold with the exception of three properties. The first is that it is found mostly on the surface of the ground, fooling those who discover it. Secondly, it tarnishes — unlike true gold. Lastly, it is as brittle as a light stone because it is merely made up of minerals which coat the outside surface of the gravel.

Pyrite is sadly representative of shallow relationships that refuse to go beyond the surface. To do so would only serve to disturb the dirt that rests just beneath the physically attractive level of all relationships. But if you desire a true and lasting relationship, you are going to have to be content with digging deep — for that is where the twenty four karat gold called true love resides. God the Father placed gold, diamonds, silver and some of the most precious minerals and oil deep within the earth's protective mantle. God also placed your greatest wealth — your heart and spirit — deep within your chest cavity. That is why the Creator judges us by the heart and not the surface. You will neither have a true relationship with anyone of the opposite gender unless you see them as God does first.

"He who values
merely surface beauty
over true love heaps his wealth
upon an ever depreciating assets."

— *Charles Rivers*

The human species, on the other hand, is more impressed with surface beauty but is dismayed once that beauty fades like the surface of pyrite. Others run once they find out that dirt is under that shallow pyrite. But mankind is not consistent in its nature of surface love. For man will run out on a relationship that presents trouble for him beyond a set limit of time. It becomes not worth the effort, sweat and toil to see it through to the gold. But if you take this same man and put him in charge of a gold mine, he will move a mountain of dirt for fifteen years, straight through some of the harshest and life threatening conditions for less than an ounce of gold.

It's intriguing that men and women both are impressed when it takes fifteen years to dig one bar of gold out of the side of a mountain. But far impressive still is our God, who would stick that same bar of gold up to one half mile deep into that mountain's side. God has buried in you treasures that may take years to find, depending on how much dirt you are willing to remove. But first each of us must be willing to venture deeper than the level of fool's gold to where the true fortune lies.

How Do I get My
Spouse to Yield Their Gold?

There is a knowledge to all living things that are under the essence of God's natural creation. If you understand what is similar to all, you can receive gold from anything that God has naturally made. Nothing under the natural created hand of the Father's love will reveal itself to you unless you passionately love it first. The reason for this is because God made those things passionately in love and in passionate love only can they be activated. The bible explains to us in Genesis 1:31 the feeling of contentment God had for what he created in the earth, "*And God saw everything that He had made, and behold, it was very good and He approved it completely.*" So if you are in the company of one of God's creations and you disapprove of it, then it will not yield to you its abundance. This premise holds the same whether it is a human, an animal or vegetation.

Have you ever tried to grow a plant without love and have it prosper? At the same time, you could live next door to a neighbor who loves plants and has the ability to grow eight foot petunias from a dying mass that stretches into your property line? Have you ever tried to keep a tank of gold fish only to have them die on you a school at a time, time and again, while a friend of yours is successful at not only getting their fish to live for years on end but breeding them with little or no effort? Have you ever been in a relationship with someone that is unfruitful for you, yet the next person in that person's life is able to have them bear much fruit? In fact you might witness that same person moving into a large-sized home, having two children, and becoming very successful.

These are the people who are very successful at knowing how to release the gold in all they come in contact with. These are God's people who could bring a starving dog from the brink of death to a fat pedigree winner. They could nurse a dying bush from a stick to lush leaves and full aromatic blooms. More importantly, they could adopt an abused child, who has a very derogatory attitude, and turn him or her around to being the most positive and fruitful person on the face of the earth. Jesus Christ himself exhibited this same passion for all the people he touched while on his earthly mission. With each individual person Jesus healed, he did so with love for them and not formulas, tricks or tactics. Jesus Christ was living proof that you will never heal or strengthen any relationship purely through the mind of man.

The bible notes, in several instances, that the bearing of fruit is a prosperous existence for mankind or agriculture. The bible also recognizes that if God's creations do not bear fruit they are either not planted in the right location or they are estranged from their creator. So all you need to learn right now is how to move your relationship to the right spiritual garden to grow, such as Adam and Eve possessed in the Garden of Eden. To do this, you will have to come to the realization that there is so much more to be changed in you than you could ever hope to achieve in changing your spouse.

Prepare yourself first to be healed if you will ever muster the will to heal your relationship. I want you to ask yourself the question that follows in italics from an honest loving heart rather than a defensive posture. If you read it this way you will feel the hurt and pain of a lifetime lift immediately from your consciousness.

> *"If my spouse was currently my*
> *best friend in the world, could I*
> *get away with treating my spouse*
> *the way I do now or would I*
> *myself have to change?"*
>
> — *Charles Rivers*

Now if you took this calling to heart then you can successfully compare the way you treat your best friends to the way you relate to your spouse. Countless persons all across the globe, like yourself, get people to do just about anything by being a true friend over being an enemy to them. Can you imagine that one child can get another to jump off a high ledge with a skateboard just because he is a best friend? Do you realize with a mere suggestion one friend can get another to go through college and complete a doctorate degree? You too can have the power to grow that plant from death or activate the life in your spouse if you love them from the heart as two friends love one another.

Why Do Christian Couples Drift Apart?

Once Christian couples decide to get married and merge homes together something secular takes place between them. In their newlywed minds, they begin to wonder out aloud about future events. One is concerned about retirement, some forty plus years away. A wife begins to vocalize how they need a larger home and better community standards for a child who has yet to be conceived. These ideas towards the future are beautiful and innocent enough, but not when they take on a life that will eventually overshadow the marriage relationship itself.

The very security a Christian family sets out to attain can become the same goal that undermines the entire family. A newlywed husband takes on as many additional hours at work for as much extra income as his job will allow an entire staff. He seeks to provide a higher standard of living for his family then the level he married at. What the husband does not cover financially, his wife can more than cover with overtime at her job. Now the couple who once had love for one another that was not based on finances begins to base their future love and happiness on money. They are proud to know that not only can they afford a new house but everything they ever dreamed possible to go into that new home.

This behavior is what I refer to as building the *Tower of Babel* to heaven in your own home. Once intelligent people lean too heavily upon the concept of believing that wealth creates heaven, every item purchased becomes a brick contributing to the height of that tower. The residents of Babel did not want to wait to get to heaven. They were insistent upon having heaven and earth at the same time. They became no longer interested in the trip as much as the destination. This is the same fallacy of couples who are future — focused and present — dead.

But God the Father does not believe in shortcuts. It was for this reason that he cut not only the tower but the residents of Babel short of their victory. They were spread apart to the four corners of the globe with confounding languages (*Genesis 11:1-3*). This is why I encourage couples to live marriage as God made it clear to them before he destroys their tower and confounds their communication.

Two years further down that same *Tower of Babel* road and the realities of how much money it will require turns that couple's dreams into a nightmare. Outrunning the interest on all of those new purchases brings depression and bickering for that once newlywed couple. The purchases they were making to enrich their own lives are doing little more than enriching the lives of the corporations they purchased them from. In fact, the more wealth they reach for without God the more impoverished their real love becomes. Now don't get me wrong — there is absolutely nothing wrong with acquiring wealth or nice things. But if we travel together on a journey called marriage and get lost along the way, we forget what the trip is truly about.

When that happens, we are no longer committed to one another in a relationship but to what we owe the creditors and most certainly to the whims of our employers, who have become the middlemen to finance our debts. Once the job becomes more important than the relationship, it will be easily said that Johnny and Jane are two very dull people. It will take a major calamity or an illness at this point before a couple feels that they can sever their ties to a job to support one another as they should. But this is not God's way, for in Deuteronomy 8:3 it states, *"And he humbled you with manna, which you did not know nor did your fathers know, that he might make you recognize and personally know that man does not live by bread only, but man lives by every word that proceeds out of the mouth of the Lord."*

In this biblical passage a golden nugget is revealed in that although we toil for material items and food, all of these things can be taken away from us. The passage clearly states that man should live by every word that proceeds from the mouth of God. So if we live for our jobs instead of our spouses, we live out of the will of God. This is a rebellious spirit similar to what a child has for his mother. If the child would just take her advice, he would be alright. But in a rebellious state, children will go all around Robin Hood's bond to take credit for doing things themselves — only to fall flat on their face.

Finally the child does exactly what the mother told him from the start and is shocked to find out it was easier and more prosperous than the route he chose. The bible does not instruct couples to make wealth king in your life. If we live God's purpose and his love, he tells us that wealth will be provided by him.

This is the primary reason why we drift out of love: we drift out of God. The proper way to wealth is given in Matthew 6:33, *"But seek (aim at and strive after) first of all His kingdom and His righteousness (His way of doing and being right) and then all these things taken together will be given you besides."* So what becomes ruinous to our love as Christian couples is that we do things our way by seeking first the kingdom of jobs, then these things are added unto us and shortly thereafter taken from us.

One reason Christian couples forsake God for money is because they watch secular couples get rich without God. I am asked often why secular couples get away with wealth when Christian couples struggle doing right. To those people, I say this: it is quite simple, for you see a Christian family will sacrifice for their family while a secular spouse sacrifices their family. Just as sure as Jesus was a sacrifice for our souls on Calvary, a secular family's soul and love become a sacrifice for an hourly wage. In the end, you will be surrounded by that which you focused your efforts on. What will that look like in your life: a wealth of acquiring or the wealth of love that never tarnishes even beyond the grave?

*Observe
from the senses
what your spouse's wants,
desires, pains and tribulation of the
heart really are. This will become a lifetime
journey that cannot be shortened for quick
answers any more than your own searching for
understanding can be. In observing someone
outside of self you can grow to understand
self and the changes that must take
place within each of us.*

Book 2

Leave
Observe
Volunteer
Evolve

*"The mind understands what
the heart refuses to, while the
heart deduces what the mind
may never comprehend."*

— *Charles Rivers*

The Secret to Living Happily Ever After

In this the book, *Observe,* I am going to reveal to you how to improve your relationship with the God-given tools that we all possess but have become estranged to. No relationship on the face of this earth reaches the age of understanding without friendship as its base. As written in the book of Genesis, Adam and Eve are not long a couple in the Garden of Eden before friendship is commanded of them. Genesis 2:24 states, "*It is not right that man should be alone, therefore a man shall leave his father and mother, unite to his bride and cleave to her and the two shall become one flesh.*"

The key to Adam's happiness or the modern day male is in deciphering this one authoritative verse. God is an awesome God indeed and he knew, long before all of the books that social scientists write concerning relationships, what to do to keep love alive within his creation. For this reason, most marriages don't have to go beyond this verse to heal any rift a modern marriage has to offer — because normally after understanding this verse many people will come to know that they were only married by law before reading it.

The day you understand it is the first day of marriage, regardless of if you have been married one or one hundred years. This is precisely the reason why most of what social science has done over the past half century towards marriage has failed. For their methods in their original intent were not created in love but are tactics in response to a hurting human reaction. Science seeks to manage the pains that humans have, where the Father seeks to liberate us from those troubles.

You see, no relationship between men and women (that has thrived about eight thousand years before modern day psychology) will be fixed by anything other than information directly from the maker's manual (the Bible). The creator also knew that as men we would become pretty much bull headed in our relationships towards our wives. It would be a difficult proposition at best for a man to keep a marriage together unless we applied this verse to our relationship.

Any Man That Cleaves In Faith Wins His Wife's Affections and Love for a Lifetime

Let us understand the methodologies of the Father's chemistry of love. This is self evident by breaking down Genesis 2:24. It states, *"Therefore a man shall* unite *to his wife,* (the word *unite* involves the marriage ceremony only) *and cleave to her"* (the word cleave involves far more than just sticking close to her). The definition of cleave in the English translation means to remain faithful. A further clarification involves being steady in affection, loyal and a faithful friend.

So cleave, as directed by the Father, meant for Adam to be steady in allegiance and a close friend to his wife. Not the run of the mill average friendship, but one that would stand head and shoulders above the strongest outside of the home relationship. The capstone of this verse is revealed when it is for told that after cleaving to her, *"the two shall become one flesh."* The couple would draw to become one as physical bodies in line with their needs and limitations, as opposed to the soul, mind or spirit. The final stage of marriage would be in loving one another as God loves us, which cannot be achieved through friendship love alone.

For even friendship love on its best day can change with the stresses of life. But it is when friendship love is buffeted by Agape love that any hurt feelings can be forgiven and people can be understood for who they are and not what they say and do in pain. So our heavenly father knew full well that just the wedding ceremony alone would not make two people a great couple. What would make an unbreakable bond is a friendship allegiance over time in line with pains, troubles and built in differences. That is the lynch pin of the verse when it is says that we become one flesh. The word *become* does not represent an immediate act, but an over time manifestation of events.

The Chemistry of Love

Each time I teach a class on relationship happiness I am always inadvertently asked one question: "Why can't men and women start relationships out as friends?" The answer to this question lies in the fact that God directs us in a path of true love that ultimately leads us back to Him. God's ultimate prize will be with his children possessing Agape love, so anything less than that is directed by the individual. Since the Father only looks out for our best interests, he would send you Agape love in the form of people your entire life and yet we prefer the Erotic type of love. That is why most people have difficulty finding God, themselves or that fantasy marriage until they live out the only love he intended for us.

Most couples start out at the first love passionately but fewer and fewer graduate to the last. I believe this to be due to the fact that over the last half century people are moving away from God's love towards a form of self love. But ultimately self love will abandon people, leaving them lonely in the heart and lonely in the end, while God's true love allows people to be surrounded by a loving family and true friends now and through their last days. Many of us balk at giving up the Erotic type of love for God's love because we feel we have something to lose. Actually, if we don't progress beyond the one love, we will know only loss in our human relationships. For couples who cannot see their spouse as God's love sees them can only see them as tools to use or objects towards a goal.

I challenge anybody who thinks that moving towards God and harmony as loss to libido to try these three loves in conjunction to one another. You will find out that no level of religiosity will ever kill your sex drive within a committed relationship. These three loves are defined from the Greek language as *Eros love*, (sexual love or desire). *Philia love*, (A friendship love arriving from close association), and *Agape love*, (Existing as the love God has for man and mankind for God and other humans). Once two people decide that they are interested in one another they experience feelings based in Eros love or an erotic-type infatuation. Men and women alike have a tendency to focus on romantic love as all encompassing, but this is merely the start of love's bloom.

Eros or sexual love is a very poor substitute for real love. Although it provides a fine start for a young couple's blossoming relationship, it makes for a bad ending if they insist on making this love primary over the last two. Any relationship that is based purely on Eros love will end with the waning of this love or once someone more attractive comes along. We must not see these three loves as separate and apart, but as a bridge to final relationship success.

Bridging the Gender Communication Gap

The longest road all relationships must cross in order to find ultimate happiness passes over the bridge of Philia love. The same path must be taken for those who seek to go from a secular life to an eternity in heaven with the Father. Are you prepared to cross the bridge to arrive at the other side to a beautiful life on earth and an eternal life thereafter in heaven?

The two opposing anchors of the bridge of friendship we must cross are Eros love and Agape love. They hold up the bridge span of Philia love. The second love God gave to mankind is Philia love or a friendship-type love. Understand that graduating to a higher level of love does not mean that you have to disregard the previous. No — in fact, you incorporate one into the other until they are seamless. The reason your love should seek to endeavor above Eros is because any relationship that is more passionate in the horizontal then vertical does not sustain itself.

The support span of Philia or friendship love, as interpreted in English, becomes the healing point that all relationships that have languished too long in an erotic road must cross. In this stage of your relationship you must exercise the same type of dynamic love, care and kindness that you extend to your other friends. Philia love should be used as a guide towards your final destiny, which is a relationship based upon the Father's love. Philia love, although more of a communicative love, should never be seen as a final destination.

The final destiny to strive for in your relationship is Agape love. Agape love is what older couples the age of our great grandparents needed to make it to death they did part. Agape love is the purest, non-sexual love in nature. It is the love that God extends towards man and man reciprocates towards God and his fellow human beings. This is the type of love that will forgive any misgivings, large or small, as surely as God forgives us. This love is equivalent to how we extend forgiveness to our out-of-the-home best friends when they wrong or slight us.

A Conniption of Loves

*"Most people
who have world class
relationships with friends
struggle at basic communication
with their spouse."*

— *Charles Rivers*

I was once asked by a man how we were supposed to be friends with our spouses when were married to them. He believed that marriage itself was enough to cover all ills and communication from two strange persons that join together. That any negative behaviors can be overlooked because we are under a marriage covenant. But his reasoning for withholding the best of his love did not jive with the way he treated almost everyone else. You see, God did not give us all three loves to parcel out as we deemed necessary.

Never was the intention to love God in one way, your spouse in another, and your friends in a separate fashion. This is a schizophrenic way of dividing up your consciousness. All three loves are needed in a combined fashion to make our marriages mature into a reflection of true love. If we offer only erotic love to our spouses, friendship love to the world, and Agape love to God, we become little more than character actors upon the stage of conditional love.

Bring Your Relationship Above the Belt if it is to Last

Couples that are facing constant strife and division at home must be prepared to move their relationship to higher ground. In fact, each unresolved issue we face in marriage is in some shape, form or fashion a cry to move our love to new levels. Let me take a moment to explain to you why this is so true. Judge for yourself all of the long term relationships you have ever had in your life: your coach, your best teacher, the preacher your best friend. All of these relationships were non-sexual in nature. It is impossible to have true forgiveness for anyone that you have only sexual feelings for.

It was the interpersonal relationships that made the longest lasting impressions upon our lives and spirit. All of the people we allowed into our lives to share a friendship relationship were able to impart wisdom, laughter or add balance to our life. Why? Because it is within the Philia relationship that you and I can be motivated to change our thoughts and opinions about one another and about life.

Now contrast this with all of the dating and sexual relationships you experienced with the opposite gender. Did you learn half as much or anything long range from those types of Erotic relationships? Why not? Because you will never be able to successfully connect your feelings and open-mindedness to a purely physical relationship. In fact, you will remain at the whims and controls of your thoughts and body chemistry over a true higher calling to love.

Why Do People Drift to the Siren Song of Erotic Love?

Unfortunate for people who buy into this type of Erotic relationship don't realize that they are sure to fail if they insist on taking them long range. Advertising seeks to sell you Eros love because it grabs the attention of the viewers' minds when a product cannot sell easily on its own. Erotic love works as a good selling tool in a rush, rush society because it is short term — and in America we love short term. But Philia and Agape love are long term and you can not readily sell a quick society on long term.

Sex Enhances the Marriage
But Divides the Dating Pair Bond

"In Agape, one can
not be in love as much as
one becomes love."

— Charles Rivers

Some people come to believe that sex ruins the friendship between men and women. That may be so for single couples who date, but it is the exact opposite for married couples who are in trouble. Never were the strengths of these loves being taught more important then when I had to counsel a minister's wife who had, over time, come to despise her husband for his attitude about the past.

She confessed she had moved out of their shared room to take up residence down the hall with her teenage daughter. She said she didn't mind being married to him as long as they stayed in separate rooms and did not have a physical relationship. Especially, she said if it meant him keeping his hands off of her. Oddly enough, she felt she still loved God with all her heart. She baked and cooked for the church on a weekly basis, while supporting other people with their lives in the church.

I explained to her the three forms of God-given love and how it would be virtually impossible for her to hate her husband on the one hand and love God on the other. Because if she had achieved love for God, being the Agape love level, she could not in good conscious turn to her husband and have none. For if people have truly reached an Agape level of love, they have learned to respect all people despite their behaviors. They have learned what it means to love people outside of their comfort zone. A person at an Agape love level of consciousness understands what was meant in the biblical quote, *"for all have fallen short of the glory of the kingdom of heaven."* This verse alone indicates that God knew we were imperfect and so we should not judge each other in this context.

Additionally, if we hate anyone outside of ourselves, we hate God himself. Why? For in Genesis 1:26, God says, *"Let us {Father, Son, Holy Spirit] make mankind in our image.* In Genesis 1:27 we are given further clarification of this image of beauty. We are told, *"So God created man in his own image, in the image of God created he him; male and female created he them."* It is proof positive; I believe that if you look at anyone with anything less than Agape, you hate not only him but his Creator as well. For one cannot hate the creation of a thing without hating its creator.

So in being indifferent to her husband and loving anywhere else her conflict rested within herself and not by anything he could do. Not only did she find fault with her husband, but the structure of marriage. If only she was aware that she was sending God the message that she disbelieved in two of his creations, [man and marriage] but that she loved herself. God will not honor any relationship in this form of religious double standard. Our heavenly Father would not be true to his word if he honored your dishonoring of the union of his creation.

In Galatians 6:6-8, it states, "*Do not be deceived and deluded and misled; God will not allow Himself to be sneered at (scorned, disdained, or mocked by mere pretensions or professions, or by His precepts being set aside.) [He inevitably deludes himself who attempts to delude God.] For whatever a man sows that and that only is what he will reap.*"

God the Father is love and since we are of God's creation we are love if we abide in the faith. But if we live by the demonstrative examples set by Satan we become what Jesus called Abraham's descendents, "*Children of the devil.*" In addition, we are told further in 1 John 3:9-11, "*This is how we know who the children of God are and who the children of the devil are: Anyone who does not do what is right is not a child of God; nor is anyone who does not love his brother.*"

> *"Become the love*
> *you desire from a person,*
> *and that person will desire to*
> *be loving around you."*

> — *Charles Rivers*

Anyone that is at one of the three levels of love should move cautiously to the next. These levels of love are growth levels and not multiple chess moves. Anything beyond Eros love cannot be achieved by either trickery or tactics scheduling of your behaviors. One should not try to skip from Eros love to Agape because they will surely face failure. It took an enjoyable learning process of some years for my wife and I to transition from an Eros relationship to a Philia love. It would take us another two years to achieve true understanding through Agape love. So give your relationship and your spouse time to grow and remember what I told you: there is no challenge in loving someone who loves you back.

As we freely accepted our mother's love as children, surely we can freely give it away to our spouses, who may be love-challenged at this point in their life. Understand that there are other forces that you will face to ruin your relationship that at times will be unseen. The bible tells us in Ephesians 6:12, "*For our struggle* is not against flesh and blood, but against the rulers, against the authorities, against the powers of this dark world and against the spiritual forces of evil in the heavenly realms." As a couple, know that long before Satan separated Adam and Eve from God, he separated Eve from Adam. The devil does not enjoy a day off to honor the Sabbath any more than he will take a day off from wreaking havoc on your marriage.

Still not Assured on Friendship?

Let us magnify the only two titles mentioned in the bible concerning husband and wife. The first is the word *companion* spoken of many times in the old and new testaments. In Malachi 2:14 it states, *"She is your companion and wife of your (marriage) covenant."* You might notice how in the verse the two titles are distinct. It recognizes that the husband and wife are friends and married at the same time. The definition of the word companion is the same as the definition of the word friend. The other definition used in the bible is to represent a spouse is *helpmeet* or in the English language *helpmate*. The definition of the word helpmeet or helpmate is exactly the same as the word friend.

Love is not conceited; it is not rude and does not act unbecoming. Love does not insist on it's own rights or it's own way. For it is not self seeking; it is not touchy or fretful or resentful.

1 Corinthians 13:5

Surrender Your Need to Control

"To be
controlling of others
one must first surrender his
or her own freedoms."

— *Charles Rivers*

One of the monumental issues that couples face in their Christian homes is not a financial one or a sexual one, as is played out in the popular media. Couples' largest problems stem from control, a tug of wills over who will be in charge of the homestead. In a home that is out of God's will a husband will try to control the relationship by force while the wife will try to control it by manipulation. Neither of these negative means used to achieve positive outcomes are the will of God. The bible tells us in Ephesians 5:23, *"That man is the head of the wife as Christ is the head of the church."*

That being said, I have had a field day instructing husbands who have misinterpreted the authority God has placed in them to guide their families successfully. In my classes I teach husbands and wives how the family of God knits together well by authority, humbleness and submission. For the one who abides in God's kingdom without submitting to authority draws condemnation and correction to their person. So if you wish to live your entire life without true happiness, this is definitely the way to get on God's bad side. If your relationship is not working for you, then God is not welcome in your home. In this book entitled "Observe", I am going to show you how to change your relationship to where it calls down great favor, mercy and the blessings of God.

In Genesis 3:16, Eve is told that, *"Thy desire shall be for your husband and he shall rule over you."* Understanding the proper application of the word [rule] helps to diminish arguments as well as conflicting philosophies in your home. The definition of rule in a relationship is meant for governance and not control or domination. Let us analyze this further, for this definition has a much broader picture of governing. All of us are under the rule or governance of someone or some organization, but ultimately God. If, as a man, you could take a hold of this study, you could dramatically change the tempo of your relationship with your wife overnight.

As men and women citizens of varying countries, we exist under our government's rule. The design of some countries' constitutions is such that the rule is unobtrusive. Laws given to maintain peace and order will not concern you unless you do not follow their governance. Now on the other hand, some foreign communist-type governments have governance structures in which they are very obtrusive on the citizens' freedoms. In these countries not only do the leaders suspend several of the citizens' basic freedoms, but they restrict access outside of the country, making it a virtual prison for all but them.

"If you make rules on
your relationship, you transition
from spouse to cop in monitoring and
policing of those sets of laws."

— *Charles Rivers*

These leaders end up becoming wardens of a prison of their own creation. In an attempt to crush their citizens' free will they have severely restricted their own. In all situations where you imprison free will, the citizens ultimately rebel. This situation is the same whether we are referring to a country, a city or your personal home. Even the hardest-hearted men who insist on reconstructing God's meaning for rule believes in free will for himself. He understands that people from all oppressed nations run, paddle or fly to free countries to be free under a more respective rule.

Now I am not suggesting for one minute that God meant for your home to be run like a democratic government, but he also did not mean to grant your wife free will for you to imprison it. When you place rules on one another, you will end up exchanging freedoms that keep your free will in check. I was asked recently by an acquaintance, who is an art dealer, why the husbands seemed to disagree with their wives on the choice of paintings.

She was also miffed why some of the wives who shopped alone insisted they had to get their husbands opinions before making a purchase. Since she had been burned by the institution of marriage through divorce she believed these wives should buy what they wanted regardless of what their husbands thought. I could understand her point of view if I analyzed relationship issues from a position of bad experiences or the preference of one gender over another.

But I told her that I could show her what she could not see if she would allow me. Once she agreed, I told her it would have been better if those wives mentioned to their husbands that they hated a particular painting that they actually liked. Then their husbands would have been sure to sway his own opinion to like and purchase it. She said, "I never looked at it that way before."

I further explained to her that the reason they needed their husbands' permission was because somewhere down the line in their marriage history she restricted either his purchase ability or an idea that was near to his heart. Now when it comes to something important to her, he is exercising his veto power. Examples of this are where one spouse tells the other I expect you back in two hours. Now the spouse that has made this rule now has to go by their own rule as to not seem like a hypocrite.

*"You can get anything you want in
life if you are just willing to help
enough people get what they
want in life."*

— Zig Zigler

I am sure that all men, including myself, enjoy the freedoms of this free society. That is why we get absolutely unnerved when we see those blue and red lights flashing in our rearview mirrors and infringing on our freedoms. As men, we get absolutely bent out of shape at the employer who tries to crush our spirit so hard that all you can dream of is the day you can find a better job or go into business yourself. This is negative governance in many forms.

I have counseled many decent men who have had a problem fighting with their wives over governance of their sanctified homes. They insist that they are trying to maintain authority, but to that I say if you have to scream and fight you have already lost authority. Your family should enjoy your governance and look forward to your leadership and input in life, and not want to run away from it. Ask yourself: is your leadership reminiscent of the former Soviet Union or a free will respecting nation?

God Throws Adam a Curve Ball

Most Christians can agree that God is the same God from Genesis through Revelations. His word is permanent and lives with us each day. We know that God's word is eternal for the bible tells us that, *"God is not a man that he should lie, nor a son of man that he should change his mind."* If you can agree on this much you should also know that when he gave Adam the gift of free will it was also extended to Eve. The gift of free will has never been rescinded from man even to this day.

He did not say, "Adam, I will give thee free will — but Eve I will not!" Just as Adam, all women have the freedom to choose right or wrong in the sight of God. God does not have us on puppet strings for he gave us both free will as opposed to guarded will. Add this gift to the mix of a home where the male is supposed to be the head of the wife and you can get for yourself some very interesting moments.

God believes in free will. You will find that when it is stated that a wife should either be subject or be submissive to her husband it is a request and not a demand. In Ephesians 5:21 wives are asked to, *"Be subject to your husband as (a service) to the lord."* But if you read further in Ephesians 5:25 husbands are asked to, *"love your wives as Christ loved the church and gave himself up for her."* This is sacrificing not as in just a job for income for your physical life. But also the life that made you an individual, our selfish lives *(and gave himself up for her.)*

Some of the religious shout down other Christians who have one foot in the church and the other in the world as hypocrites. But I say to you that Jesus instructs us that the covenant of marriage is a church. So if we have one foot in marriage and the other in single life, does this not make us hypocrites to that church?

If a church is doing wrong in teachings, its members (*children and family*) will fall away from it. If the church of marriage is not doing right in its teachings not only will it lose the members but it will serve to scare others away from being converts. Today we find that if people are not satisfied with their marriage they will exchange it as easily as they do one Christian church for another.

This entire biblical passage frames the institution of marriage between men and women. The bible never insists that a wife do something solely that it does not direct the husband to graciously mirror. A wife should submit to her husband as a member of the church called home as man must submit his authority to Christ. If a man is not willing to submit authority to Christ, he should not expect his wife to submit to his authority.

> *"Never expect anyone*
> *to do something that you*
> *are not willing to do*
> *first yourself."*

> — *1SG. Louise A. Montero*

Look now at a similar example given in Colossians chapter 3 verses 18-21. It begins with instruction to wives, *"Wives be subject to your husbands, as is right and fitting and your proper duty in the Lord." 19. Husbands, love your wives and do not be harsh or bitter or resentful toward them.* Finally the behavioral role of the children in a Christian home is identified. *20 Children, obey your parents in everything, for this is pleasing to the lord.* Note the only command given was to the child of the home as in [children, obey]. Never is it suggested that the wife obey the husband as a child would a parent.

In describing the family's harmony, he instructs the relationship of the father to the children. *21. Fathers, do not provoke or irritate or fret your children, lest they become discouraged and sullen and morose and feel inferior and frustrated.* In other words, do not break their spirit. So as men we must remember that if we are bitter with our wives we deny them the very same choices we enjoy most. That choice is to follow freely in subjection as he instructs men and everyone in the body of Christ. If we provoke our children, we risk making them wayward in the world we seek to keep them safe from.

In 1 Peter 2:13 all Christians are told, *"Be submissive to every human institution and authority for the sake of the Lord, whether it be to the emperor as supreme."* Now how many of us men can say we have, as Christians, successfully submitted without question to the will of all of our governing authorities? As men we must honor our wives' submission as a gift and not a right in order to be blessed by it. To receive this precious gift as a husband, you must yourself come under God's authority. For only under God's authority will you do right in your dealings and communications with your family. Otherwise, if we seek to draw authority from any place else but God, where must that authority originate?

The Strength of Submission, the Weakness of Rebellion

"For the rebellious person swims against the tide of their own God given compassions."

— *Charles Rivers*

This chapter is written specifically to Christian wives who have been struggling with submitting to their husbands in Christ. I encourage you not to fight your husbands on every suggestion they offer, particularly when he is living correctly in the governance of his home as directed by God. This behavior serves little more than to de-convert you and your spouse and to cause your behavior to become as demonic as the husband who would lead his home as a tyrant. Husbands who seek to depart a marriage through divorce usually report a sense of being unwelcomed by their wives prior to their departure from the marriage.

This does not mean that their wives actually told them that she did not need him, but she never showed him that his presence served any purpose outside of being a provider. This feeling of being unwelcomed must dominate the air in a home, job or neighborhood before someone flees it. This attitude of "I can do without you" is little more than rebellion of God's word disguised as opposite gendered strife. Because God has placed husbands in this position of authority by draft instead of choice, you are not fighting your husband as much as you are fighting God. Because of this type of behavior, God will not bless your home anymore than you would reward your children for their wayward behavior.

Rebellion always brings with it a call down to discipline while humbleness commands you to give favor to the obedient. But the way society behaves you would have thought it would serve you to do the reverse. If you want to find out where you are failing in life or love, determine who or what you are rebellious against. It may be your job, marriage or any place where you should have influence but you do not. People have a natural resistance to the spirit of rebellion.

If you discover an area in your life where you are prosperous and communicate well, you will find that you neither have rebellion nor resistance in that location.

Take the behaviors that you apply to your successes and apply them to the areas in life you are deficient in.

When a wife rebels against her husband she must ask herself if she is rebelling against him or all male authority in general. Does her rebellion stem from childhood dealings with the opposite gender or negative messages concerning men? Unless you forgive those men and yourself for having a negative opinion, you will destroy your own happiness. I have discovered that rebellion in the long run only affects the rebellious person. People who have a rebellious nature at home, on the job, or in society don't get promoted or trusted. They cannot be trusted to promote because they will not complete anything that was told to them by the person in authority over them without discussion or apathy.

> *"If you cannot*
> *follow then you can*
> *never lead successfully."*

> — 1SG. Louise A Montero

It is impossible for the hardened of heart rebellious person to learn because the rebellious person shuts his/her ear off to authority. A mother who rebels against the authority of her husband unknowingly teaches her children to rebel against all authority. Ultimately those same children will rebel against their own mother as she is in authority over them. A rebellious child cannot climb any ladder of success for they will be stopped by all those in authority over them.

In Ephesians 4:1, it states, *"I therefore, the prisoner for the Lord, appeal to and beg you to walk (lead a life) worthy of the (divine) calling to which you have been called (with behavior that is a credit to the summons to God's service living as becomes you) with complete lowliness of mind (humility) and meekness (unselfishness, gentleness, mildness), with patience, bearing with one another and making allowances because you love one another."*

Have you ever noticed how law enforcement identifies the rebellious person out of a group of people who are not? Yes, rebellion always calls down correction wherever it raises its head. Have you ever seen a rebellious child being removed from a classroom at school amidst a bunch of calm children? Have you ever witnessed God's wrath being poured out upon the sinner while the saints all around them went unaffected?

The bible describes, in many different forms, the rewards of the submissive or humble compared to that of the rebellious. In 1 Peter 5:5 we are told, *"For God sets Himself against the proud [and He opposes, frustrates, and defeats them], but gives grace (favor, blessing) to the humble."* In Luke 18:14, we are told, *"for everyone who exalts himself will be humbled, but he who humbles himself will be exalted."* Lastly in Psalm147:6, we are told, *"The Lord lifts up the humble and downtrodden; He casts the wicked down to the ground."*

Rebellion is one of the greatest tools in Satan's arsenal to undermine those who follow God. In rebellion Satan seeks to lift humans up against God, as he did himself, which ultimately brings the wrath of God down upon a person. The bible tells us that, *"Pride and a haute spirit come just before the fall of a person."* Satan was the first to convince man that they did not need God or his creation of marriage. He sought to convince Eve that she too would be a god if she ate of the fruit. That is precisely why God gave Adam and Eve the order of marriage authority prior to expelling them from the Garden of Eden. Not only did Adam and Eve not become gods but their position in life became lowered instead of raised for listening to the advice of a demonic angel.

Develop a Hands-On Relationship

The longest journey any one of us will take is the one back to finding who we are in the kingdom of God. View a newly coupled man and woman and you will find two people so close to one another you would have believed that they were joined together at the hip. Men in these romantic early stages of the relationship massage their wives' feet. Women in this same inspired state of early matrimony massage their men's scalps until they fall asleep in their arms like little children. Both sexes cook for one another and serve the meals in a loving way reminiscent of five star restaurants. Baths are drawn to candle lit music and rose petals are sprinkled from the tub to the bed of love making.

This is the essence of love, although an Eros relationship to start this behavior is what initially binds men and women together. When we do these types of loving actions we send our mates the message that we care for them immensely. Conversely, when we stop doing these actions over time we send them the message that we could care less. But all is not lost, even if your relationship is currently void of these behaviors. Because a lot of these gifts of love we give are not authentic to our Eros love nature. They are merely copied from romantic films, magazines and suggestions from society. So when we perform duties that are not authentic to our own behavior, over time they will fall away from our concern.

The First Romance Was Written By God

Now it is much easier to do all of these loving gestures and have them be natural to your nature — if you adopt God's meaning of love over yours. You see, God is the original inventor of love, romance and compassion. Did God the Father not make the Garden of Eden? I don't know about you, but there could not be a better place to be a natural romantic then in that type of setting. Did God the Father not present Eve to Adam? What a beautiful gift of romance to crown a Garden filled with love: a beautiful woman to share the rest of your life with. Does the Father not show us the meaning of compassion and strength through his son Jesus Christ giving his life for our sins on the cross?

Yes, long before any romantic novel, magazine or television show, the Father was in the business of romance. Most men that I counseled who had a problem connecting with their wives one on one had, over time, become estranged from her true nature. A vast majority of the women who were married to their husbands for over a decade were still puzzled by his wants and desires of his heart. I can remember men coming to me, puzzled about their wife's desires, and saying, "I don't know what women want. I mean, should I just go out and get my wife roses?" I asked this particular man how has his wife responded in the past when he shown up at the door with a surprise of roses. The reply back from this man was, "Well she just put them in a vase until they died — as if she didn't care."

I then suggested he stop bringing home the roses and give her what she really wants. "What in the world would that be?" he said. I told him that after fifteen years of marriage, no one on earth should know her as much as he should. I told him that if he would just use the five senses that God gave him with his heart instead of his brain, he would know his wife. He said, "I'm willing to play, but I'm telling you that woman is a mystery."

I bet him that he could crack that mystery in a couple of minutes where years had left him puzzled. To prove this, I gave him a simple, practical exercise right then and there. I had him sit quietly and restful in a chair before me. Then I asked him to picture the contents on the bedroom dresser they had shared for the past fifteen years. He soon had a mental picture of what I wanted his mind's eye to see. I then told him to reach out and mentally place his hand on the smallest most replenishable item that she enjoys on that dresser.

In less than five seconds he shouted out, "She likes skittles candy!" I told him that this was just the smallest of successes that he would have the ability to taste if he stopped viewing his wife as one dimensional. It is important to all people, be they secular or religious, to understand that they are not married to all women or all men. Don't generalize your focus when it needs to be narrowed, as the husband found out when it came to the skittles. For when your mind is on the entire world you could lose your car keys for an entire day only to find them later in your pocket.

Tuning in the Five Senses of Love

Our five senses are utilized at each level of love from Eros to Agape. Most people out of touch with the last two levels of love lean more upon the sexual cues of the first. In an Eros relationship where there is sexual contact we use heightened senses of hearing, sight, touching, taste and smelling. But this is not the best that love has to offer; in fact, it is the very least that love can hope to offer up through the senses. Shortly after the act of love making is over, all five of these senses can subside to a less than nonchalant attitude between the participants. A couple that can be in tune in sex may not hear, see, touch, taste through physical contact anymore then sensing one another through smell afterwards.

Not one of the three spiritual levels of love God created operates as it should without the five senses being active. The only difference is that for each level of love you climb to, your senses grow from narrow-minded to spirit-minded. If you want to graduate your senses beyond the erotic level to the Philia level of communication you must master hearing your spouse as the person they are and not the person you wish them to be. If you can grow to accomplish this you will be able to physically touch them without having them withdraw from you. They will invite you into their world to taste how they see life. Your senses will become heightened to smelling out pleasures or troubles in your relationship.

At the highest level of the senses, Agape love, your closeness will be akin to standing in the presence of God. As a spouse you would have attained the *hearing* of the soul of the person you share a covenant with. You will have achieved the *sight* of God when it comes to viewing your spouse as one of God's beautiful creations, regardless of if they are in a good mood or unpleasant one. You will have the God-given influence to *touch* their life and expand their influence as you never did before. As an Agape Christian couple you will be able to *smell* the victory God intends for you long before it is visually manifested. Most importantly, you will be able to *taste* the victories denied to you when you were in the infancy of love or an Eros relationship.

Learning To Listen With the Heart

The only way two friends anywhere on planet earth associate with one another is by listening with the heart by way of their ears. If you communicate with anyone focusing merely on their auditory skills in association with the brain, your message will be lost in translation. For when communication is meant solely for the brain the listener engages the ability to filter out messages from the speaker. Listening other than with the heart is done primarily in school settings. Even in those settings if the teacher cannot grab the children's attention they risk a wave of tired eyes staring back at them. If you have ever learned from a teacher in any level of school then they touched your heart through your ears.

To listen by the heart is to equate someone's present experience with your past experience of a similar occasion until you are present in the moment with them. This is the best way to empathize with another beyond the traditional barriers of opposite gender communications. Not by cutting them off to rehash what you went through but by remembering the feeling you get in their shoes for a time. I can vividly remember sitting with wives who tell me their husbands are bored with issues that concern them. But these same men sit and listen to their friends for hours on end about the features of a new fishing rod with fast, alluring bait.

I have sat in conferences with husbands who admitted that their wives could care less about the real issues that concern them. On the other hand, these women listen for weeks at a time about their girlfriends' trials and misgivings concerning their boyfriends. If husband and wife learn to listen through the ears to the heart, you can cross gender barriers of association. Did you know that some of the best salesmen in the country communicate with you this way? It matters not that the product is a car, groceries or drugs peddled by a street junkie. The salesman bypasses your ears and goes straight for the heart. If they are good salesmen they will supply the needs of your heart. If they are bad salesmen they will manipulate you to make a quota to attain wealth.

Now if you ever came upon a salesperson who could not connect with you it was because they were trying to sell your mind through facts concerning the product. They had not attained seasoning for the position they held, just as a young husband or wife falls short in communicating. In Matthew 6:21, it says, *"For where your treasure is, there will your heart be also."* Does your spouse have your heart when he or she communicates; and if not, who does?

Learn to Stay Calm in a Tense Situation

It is written that the enemy (Satan) comes to kill, steal and destroy. But usually by the time we have learned to recognize his footprints he has done his dirty work and is well on the retreat. The tools Satan uses to get in your home are the same he has been using since the beginning of time: namely your anger, discord and strife in that order.

Did you know that the average human provides safety for themselves by driving with a seat belt on? Once the vehicle is parked at home they lock the doors and set the car alarm. Inside of the home they feel safe behind strong doors and double locks from burglars. Beyond these protections they set motion alarms prior to going to bed. Should a burglar get beyond all of these security measures, he will have to contend with the loaded weapon in the nightstand drawer. Surely we feel safe, but it is a false sense of security.

For you see the most dangerous burglar has the ability to sneak into your home and take all you possess. He steals not only goods, but your life. That criminal is the devil and he easily bypasses all of man's protective measures. Why? Because once we feel safe we leave the doors of our minds wide open to attack. We disarm the security and put away our weapons (the Bible). Eliminate the devil's ability to invade your home through your mind and you are well on your way to evicting him from your Christian marriage.

How to Avoid a Collision of Opinions

No matter whether we are talking about cars on a busy street, boats on a crowded lake, or couples in an aggravated situation, when two objects meet each other without any clear authority on how to yield, a collision will occur. Each time we argue with our spouses we are trying to hold our ground on our personal reasoning. This is the chemistry for all disagreements: we only fight for our right of way and refuse to acknowledge the other person's right to an opinion. Cars use traffic to yield, boats use right of ways. For humans, the clear yield sign in a conflict is respect.

If you lack respect, you will only hear your own opinion bouncing off of the person you are drowning out. We respect our friends' opinions when they are wise or when it is otherwise. We even side with them if they have a better opinion then ours. Couples who have lost respect for one another and refuse to yield in a discussion come to marriage counseling to have us play traffic cop. It becomes our job to stand guard over a broken traffic signal and ensure that husband and wife yield at the communication traffic intersections. But playing cop to two aggressive conversation drivers is never a permanent solution to disrespect in a marriage.

So instead I make each spouse aware of the root cause of their behavior so they can change it. When I have a couple where the husband or wife exclaims they hate their spouse, I show them how this estranges them from God. For when we hate our spouses we not only sin against God but against our own humanity. To understand how, you must first understand the statement, "I hate my husband." A wife reveals her true un-Godly nature when she says *I hate*. It truly does not matter whether she placed the words *my husband* at the end of that declaration or something else. The declaration of the spirit has come through the mouth of the messenger.

When we profess hurtful statements like these we reveal our true painful nature that is masked by our pleasant demeanor. No one can be all loving and yet all hating at the same time; that person will live in constant conflict inside of themselves. Usually when we get angry at our spouse it is not because of what they have done but because of what has been done to us prior to marrying them. Our anger grows from a small spark inside that, if left unchecked, grows into a raging flame. That spark may begin with just a fleeting comment from another person in your work environment. Combine work stress with a two hour traffic jam and you will be primed for a prickly nature.

Why are we so susceptible to anger from others? Because human nature is geared in such a way that we are sponges to the environment we inhabit. If we spend an entire day in a pleasant, loving environment, we absorb that love and come home with the ability to squeeze out that level of love. But if we have occupied a negative, energy-draining environment, we come home and wring out all of that pain over our personal relationships and ourselves.

Once we arrive home and get into a difference of opinion with our spouse it will begin with a *thought*. "I can't believe you said that to me," goes off in your head. The mind now grows in anger as we come into what I call *inthoughtsified*. This means even after your difference of opinion has passed you continue to stew internally. "Why would she say that to me? Look at all I have done for her! Why I was with her when no one even cared." These thoughts leave two adults sleeping in two separate rooms and ignoring one another for days on end.

While resting in separate spaces without resolution you transition to the last stage I call *inthoughtsification*. You are now drunk with thoughts of what if, why would and maybe ifs. Your mind begins to run overtime, even during sleep — if you can manage to squeeze in any. Work now takes on a whole new meaning as it becomes your respite from your spouse, whom you should have been able to lean upon for friendship and support. Both husband and wife are waiting for apologies from the other for something that did not originate from the marriage. We cannot expect our home relationships to remove what the outside world stains on a daily basis. When you are inthoughtsicated you must break your focus by realizing you are drunk with thoughts of indifference.

In your current state of indifference, the devil has gained a foothold in your home and, if you are not careful, for the rest of your life. He has slid in the front door of your sanctified home where even salesman is barred entrance. He has infiltrated your mind with frustration and thoughts of anger. In this aggravated state not only is the devil winning against God in your sanctified home, but at this level of anger you would, on a whim, trade your entire future finances, family and happiness in hopes of being single again. The enemy comes to steal, kill and destroy because divorce is such a permanent fix for a temporary problem.

When Bringing Out the Worst in You is Best For You

"Iron sharpens iron; so a man
sharpens the countenance of his friend,
[to show rage worthy purpose].

— Proverbs 27:17

During a tense counseling session I listened as a husband requested that his wife be more of a mother and a better wife to her family. His wife, seated across the table from him, wanted her husband to be more relaxed and intuitive to her feelings. I find it funny how God pulls opposites to live with one another in marriage. This leaves couples in a quandary: husband and wife find themselves asking their spouse for something they are incapable of doing.

This does not mean that they won't be able to do them at some future date, but they are currently resistant to change in this area. But if we yield out of respect to our spouses we could let go of the negatives in our life and we would be capable of concurring not only on things that our spouse does not particularly like in us but what we can't tolerate in ourselves.

This is the entire majesty of the Creator of the universe; he always places opposite strengths together to sharpen one another's weakness into newfound strengths. We are called as Christians to draw out the bitter portions of one another and replace them with love. Marriage draws out the truths in people that no other relationship is willing to address. Why even your own outside of the home friends will tolerate your negative behavior as much as they will your positive. That type of blind understanding will never bring you to change.

In fact, the wrong that our friends tolerate in us is no more than double standard behavior. If our friends caught their spouse doing what they tolerate in us they would be absolutely livid. I had a session with a wife who was absolutely angry at her husband when she believed he cheated on her. But oddly enough, she was best friends with another woman who had seven years of cheating on her husband.

Our View unto the World

Staying calm in the midst of a tense discussion will yield the most precious relationship gold imaginable. On the rainiest, coldest day of the year, when people prefer to be warm inside, someone is found splashing in puddles without a coat on. To us, maybe yesterday was the worst day of our life while someone in another part of the country was celebrating the birth of a newborn. Down the block from you, God has just answered a lifetime prayer for one of your neighbors. What we see and feel inside becomes our version of reality.

This is why, when in a tense discussion with your spouse, you should expect him or her to see a different reality from the same conversation based on the current mood. If you do not listen to your spouse in a disagreement, what is missed will be rehashed in subsequent arguments in louder tones. As a couple you must take that rebellious nature out of your relationship in order to merge as a team. The rebellious nature is such that it prevents the forming of any team before it is removed from a person or an environment. My experience in the military basic training camp is that they accept young people from all backgrounds from different parts of the country.

Now the drill instructors use basic training for one purpose mainly. They know that most of these children just left their parents' home where they openly rebelled against their authority. This means that they are the last people on earth who can make a cohesive team. The rebellion must be removed in order to merge them into a team of soldiers. What remains is self discipline, respect for the team effort and newfound honor for the parents they originally disobeyed. A large percentage of people who could not make it through basic training were never team players. So whether you are in the military, on the job, or married, you must be willing to learn the essence of a team.

Praise God for Your Differences

In relationships we are attracted to our spouses, in many cases, because they are contradictory to our own behavior. I strongly believe we are attracted to what we once found beautiful within our own nature at one time, but is now missing. A harsh man will be attracted to a free-spirited woman. Why, because he once was a free-spirited boy before he went through the trials and distractions of youth. So, in essence, he is attracted to himself, which is the core of healing in the heart of the marriage.

A woman who has no order in her life finds herself attracted to a man who is insanely neat and time focused. So we are attracted to our mates as opposites. In America, fifty percent of all first time marriages end in divorce. These marriages are mainly made up of opposite natured people. They become convinced that opposite character couplings are the death of marriage. As people enter their second marriage they tend to turn to people who are of the same nature. They set their course on a mistaken quest of harmony by finding a clone of themselves in the opposite gender.

Why are people motivated to do this? Because they are bombarded by radio, television and internet experts who seek to convince us that we should be compatible to achieve harmony in a relationship. But woe to those people who fall for this belief, because an astounding sixty-seven percent of all second marriages end in divorce and these are mainly made up of people who were looking for themselves. As humans we are akin to poled magnets, attracted by the opposite and repelled by the same when it comes to choosing a spouse.

This is why you should honor your differences during a disagreement. Just because your spouse's opinions are not yours does not mean they are wrong. Our job as Christians should be to find out how we can turn a disagreement into an agreement. Since we are attracted to the opposite, what does your spouse's mannerisms, attitudes and work ethics say about you? Do they overshadow you, revealing weaknesses you did not know you had or do they fall far short, showing that you are too work focused?

Your differences should compliment one to another. Salt and sugar (men and women) make for good baking ingredients. But if the blend of one of the two is stronger it will spoil a good recipe; it will destroy a great marriage. Despite the belief that one's life will be much better living with someone of the same character, I believe differently. For it is the people who fought the hardest to convert their spouses who end up missing all of the things that made them different.

You see, the worst thing we can do is marry someone for a difference and then switch up and try to convert them into being ourselves. To arrive successfully at Agape love for your spouse, others or God, you must end self love. What is self love? Certainly not the expression of a healthy love for yourself. This type of exclusive love occurs when you have no other love but for yourself. We are often told that "you cannot love someone else unless you first love yourself," but actually you cannot love someone else unless you first yield love of self.

What Are Some Origins of Self Love?

Since as far back as childhood, all of us want to be honored by our parents, peers and friends. When we run into a situation where we do wrong in our parents' eyes and they become disappointed in us instead of our behavior, we go out in the world to seek to recover that lost recognition. But we don't just pick anyone as a friend — we seek out ourselves. People often choose friends who look so close in appearance you could confuse them as family members.

We choose friends of like mind, character and appearance. We are seeking to find someone who will never disagree with us. We are searching for someone who won't push us out of our comfort zone. In other cases, we adapt our unique images to mirror one another. If your parents disapprove of you doing drugs or other wrong behavior, there will be a friend somewhere waiting to acknowledge your wrong as right. As parents, we can still honor the child but not the behavior. Everyone, everywhere in life seeks to be honored for who they are and perhaps where they are during a particular phase of growth in life.

If, as parents, we cannot honor our children, we inadvertently push them headlong right into the waiting arms of the negative influences we seek to keep them safe from. When we do not honor our spouses for who they are despite the behavior, we lead them into the path of sin. Have you ever noticed the pictures of bank robbers on your local news? Not only do they look exactly alike but they were friends even in the worst of situations.

We broaden self love by choosing groups of people or opinions that reflect our own thoughts and behaviors, successfully shutting out any others. It's ironic that when couples start to grow apart they begin to long for their personal past and friends. We begin to fantasize about what life could have been if we had never met up with our spouses. We have visions of a perfect life: problem-free and with financial concerns alleviated. This is a trick of the devil to take an image of something that never was and try to superimpose it over your current life.

This is the same trick he played on Adam and Eve in the Garden of Eden. Satan was the first person to separate what God had brought together. In the bible we are told by Jesus, *"What God has brought together let no man set asunder or apart."* What we fail to understand is that it takes less effort to make all of that stuff come true as a team then as an individual. When we divorce, we are doing the devil's dirty work for him without pay.

*Volunteer
to cater to your
spouse's wants and
desires of the heart without
any inhibition on your part. Seek to
understand through the healing
process their past pains and
tribulations of a once
wounded heart.*

Book 3

LEAVE

OBSERVE

VOLUNTEER

EVOLVE

"Those who learn to give of self
die to self, and broaden their
capacity to love another."

— Charles Rivers

Volunteer Your Love for Life

I have found time and time again in my dealings with couples that God the Father sends pain specific spouses in the lives of those persons who need change. These pain-specific spouses have the unique ability of meeting their mates on whatever love level they have been hurt on. Now that does not mean that these pain-specific spouses will come to you as angels.

As a matter of fact, they will usually come to the relationship with just as many concerns as you brought to the marriage. But in helping to heal their pains you will find your own easier to forgive. Unbeknownst to them, they are on a mission to free you of the pains you have absorbed or the unforgiveness you refuse to relinquish. At times, God even pairs up a set of people who can only heal one another through their opposite behavior.

People Are Wounded By Love, Not By Hate.

"Those who
make themselves
receptive to the desires of
their spouses become in their
actions most desirous."

— *Charles Rivers*

If someone has been hurt in the world, it is do to love and not hate. Do you believe that? As humans, we are disappointed at the level that people let us down on the Eros, Philia or Agape levels of love. It is much easier for us to guard our heart against hate, but it is when hate sneaks in as love that we are powerless to defend ourselves. If you are young and dating someone and you find out that they have betrayed you by having sex with someone else, you will feel hurt by Erotic love. Being betrayed at the lowest level of love usually makes people cautious about the fidelity of the opposite gender for their entire lives.

If, during your growing years, you have a friend who betrays your solemn trust, you would have been hurt by Philia love. In the future you will be cautious to letting your guard down too soon to new friends.

If you have ever been hurt by your parents and you believe the event to be unforgivable, then you have been hurt by Agape love. Since the love of family is supposed to be given by God, having mistrust in this level of love will definitely delay an individual's true path to God. Some people who have had either a death in the family or a great financial fall in their lives feel that God has betrayed them.

In exchange for what they perceive as loss of guaranteed love, they turn their backs in kind on God. They feel that God's love and protection should be guaranteed enough to prevent any tragedy from ever befalling their lives. This thinking is about as unrealistic as tragedies occurring within marriages being the fault of the unwitting participants. If God the Father allows life to carry on where we go through the valley of death and emerge on the other side, that should tell us something. We allow our spouses the benefit of the doubt when things happen on their time that remains out of anyone's control?

There is truly a connection of blame that is the same in marriage as it is for God when it comes to expectations of failed miracles. In both relationships we can feel hurt or turned away by love permanently to the detriment of our own happiness. But it depends on what we do next that shows what type of love we are really made of in the presence of pain. If we allow ourselves to get angry immediately, as Christians, then we reside in Eros love. Eros love in the body of the secular or the religious person has no patience for mistakes. But, if in the face of pain or betrayal we insist that there is a brighter day, we reside in the mindset of

Philia love. If you persist through the face of pain and discouragement in seeking the will of God, then you exist in the Agape level of love.

How Does One Redeem a Heart Once it has been Injured by Love?

*"Multiple layers of injury
necessitate multiple layers
of healing."*

— Charles Rivers

Those who have been hurt by a particular level of love must be healed by that same level of love. One who has been hurt on the Agape level of love should not expect that an erotic relationship will heal them. If you were hurt in a particular love, God will send you someone to assist your healing through that form of love. A person who has been raped or molested may be sent a person who has patience in these areas. These pain-specific people will not rush your healing process, even if they are estranged to what has happened to you. But remember that each person that God sends to be part of your healing process has been given strength to stand a limited test of their time and patience.

The first thing that most of us that have been hurt by love do is to get angry. This follows the feeling of mistrust and a vengeful spirit towards those people who failed to love us properly. This does not mean that we will take vengeance upon those persons who wronged us. But it will make future dealings painful for those who are close to reopening those wounds. To act in this manner, one must cast a blanket of blame against all persons from that same ethnic, gender or racial background. At this point we are choosing to consciously withhold love from others as it was withheld from us at that critical juncture. When we withhold God's love from people who are entitled to it, we steal something precious from them and the world.

*"Volunteerism is the enemy
of unforgiveness for it requires
that we free ourselves from
the protective trappings of
self preservation."*

— Charles Rivers

When we deny love to those closest to us, those people in turn will do the same towards people they come in contact with. Such a ripple effect can take place that will ultimately kill a family, a community and the body of Christ. The absence of love creates all conflicts. It depletes the air and suffocates the life out of any room or situation. You cannot have a war at home any more than you could between two countries without the absence of love, God's love in us.

> *"We either bring*
> *people our love or we*
> *present them with our current*
> *circumstances."*

> — *Charles Rivers*

During a bad state of mind, we withdraw love from a room just as surely as we bring love in with us in a positive mood. All of us bring one of the three loves wherever we roam. For instance, a young lady who wants to attract a young man sexually sends out signals of Eros love. That same young lady in the company of a girl friend sends out the signals of Philia love. She can then turn her behavior and attitude towards Sunday church to allow herself to feel Agape love.

Each day, just as surely as we can bring love to an environment, we can cancel out certain loves that exist within an environment. The Pope can walk into any bar where there is drinking and swearing and immediately vanquish Eros love from the room and fill it with Agape love before the lights were even turned up — that is not to say that the pontiff would ever visit any of these places.

Learning How to Forgive

> *"One who*
> *finds it hard to*
> *forgive another bases*
> *their forgiveness upon merit.*
> *They are estranged to Christ who*
> *offered all forgiveness*
> *through grace.*

> — *Charles Rivers*

For many couples, it would seem as if the loneliest time in their lives was spent in the presence of one another. Tina and John were just that type of couple; their names are changed here to give them anonymity. Tina arrived at my office frustrated, with scowl on her face that honestly went about as low as her chin. She sat for at least one hour into the session with her arms crossed defensively. She was mad and she wanted her husband to know it. Her trust for her husband had left their relationship years ago. She revealed to me that she was sure that her husband had cheated on her. Because of this, she refused to have sex with him and avoided any personal affection towards him for the last two years.

My personal mission regarding Tina's marriage would end up being threefold. To start, I would work on bringing stability to an already crumbling relationship. Secondly, I would turn the parents' focus off of selfish exploits and towards their children who sorely needed it. Lastly, but more important than the other two, I would show Tina the meaning of forgiveness for past offenses. The last part would be even more difficult by the fact that she was still smarting from knowing that her father had cheated on her mother when she was a teenager.

So, in Tina's mind, this just reaffirmed the comment she made about men being "that ninety-nine percent of them cheat around on their wives." Adultery is a hard hurt to overcome whether you are a man or a woman. But I believe that all of the doctors and therapists, counselors included, that ever walked this planet never gave us the tools to cope with this subject as much as Jesus Christ. If you are familiar with the bible, I am referring to the incident in which Mary Magdalene was being chased by the Pharisees to be stoned to death for the then crime adultery, *John 8:1-7*.

The Pharisees who planned to stone her figured that not only would they get the chance to kill Mary Magdalene but they could get Jesus if he agreed with her and broke the law given to Moses by God. The Scribes and Pharisees addressed Jesus concerning her case: did he believe she should be stoned to death? Hearing their question, Jesus turned to write in the sand and then back to address them. Jesus said, "Yes I know and agree about the laws given Moses." He then told them that, *"he who is among you that is without sin let him be the first to cast a stone at her."*

This comment, in my mind, ended the practice of stoning, for you see, one by one, the Pharisees walked away, from the eldest to the youngest, because they were convicted by their own consciences. The Pharisees may not have committed adultery, but all of them knew that they had broken one or all of God's Commandments. They knew because of this that they were the last people on earth to be able to question Mary Magdalene or anyone else for that matter. Christ then turned to Mary Magdalene to ask, *"Woman, where have your accusers gone?"* He knew that the Pharisees stood in as the jury and his job was to be the judge of this hastily assembled kangaroo court.

Mary responded to him, *"They have gone my Lord."* Christ in turn replied to her, *"Then I can judge you neither, go and sin no more."* You see the sin of adultery is just that, a sin. The sin of adultery carries no higher weight of condemnation than lying or stealing. For in Revelations 21:8 we are told, *"That even the liar will have his place in the lake of fire."*

As a teacher of the institution of marriage, I carry no cavalier attitude towards this sin than I do any other. But I tell you this and it is the truth that any home, community or nation that holds Erotic love higher than God's love will find high crimes and misdemeanors in the sin of adultery. I explained this to Tina during counseling. Adultery is one of the sins in the Ten Commandments and not the most damning one. God does not rate the Ten Commandments as man chooses to.

God the Father does not indicate any lenience towards lying while holding his ground on adultery. Knowing this, Tina could not stand in judgment of her husband anymore then the Pharisees would be able to. For in Tina's lifetime she had broken most, if not all, of the Ten Commandments. Surely she had taken God's name in vain within her lifetime.

Most definitely, in her short lifetime she had stolen and bore false witness against another. She had admitted to coveting the house, careers and vehicles of her best friends. Tina found herself with a rock in her hand against Mary Magdalene (*her husband*). I explained to Tina that forgiveness is a gift where three win. In forgiving her husband she actually becomes the first person in his life outside of his mother and God to forgive his selfish behavior. Therefore her true husband gets to receive her gift of love.

> *"One should only*
> *count themselves as*
> *healed who has first developed*
> *forgiveness in their heart towards*
> *the person they embrace the*
> *greatest hate against."*

> — *Charles Rivers*

Secondly, in her case, she actually gets to practice her love walk by forgiving her husband. But lastly God Himself benefits by her forgiveness. For we are told in Matthew 6:14 that, *"For if you forgive people their trespasses [their reckless and willful sins, leaving them, letting them go, and giving up resentment], your heavenly Father will also forgive you."* When we forgive those who have transgressed against us we dismiss the wrath that they were ultimately supposed to face from God. In Romans 12:19, *"Dearly beloved, avenge not yourselves, but rather give place unto wrath: for it is written, Vengeance is mine; I will repay, saith the Lord."*

In her angered and embittered state, she has actually given of herself to her transgressor. This is Christ-like in nature to forgive another before they deserve it, and no higher love is there. As a bonus, Tina gives herself the gift of liberation: the liberation from hatred which had its hold on her very soul for a long time. Yes, two people always benefit from the gift of forgiveness. To forgive is a gift to someone before they are worthy of it, just as God the Father forgives us before we are deserving. He does not wait until we are deserving of the gift; if He did, we would never be able to achieve it.

Tina's original problem was that she had to forgive her father for the same offense before she could forgive her husband. She had held so long to her unforgiving state that it had become part of her makeup as a human being. The excess baggage we carry through life is a living testimony to God of our unwillingness to forgive and leave the past behind. Look into your past at the people who have wronged you. Make a list if you must, but start on your personal path of forgiveness today. Unforgiveness has hurt your past, will damn your present and withdraw life right out of your future.

In the classes I teach, I have projectile ceiling lamps that I stand under for a demonstration. It is a demonstration of the light we place our spouses in. When you see your spouse as some sort of angel over a human you deny them their humanity and human frailties. Of course all humans will falter; it is their fallen nature. In the bible we are told that *"For all have sinned and fallen short of the kingdom of heaven."*

God the Father knew that we were flawed since the initial fall of man. In life, most people will carry an "anything goes" attitude with their friends because they don't want to see them pigeon-held by any rules they would impose upon them. At the same time, we carry an angel-like appearance with our spouses that will not allow them human frailties lest our full wrath be unleashed upon them.

So if we take it upon ourselves not to forgive our spouses for an offense we act outside of God's will. Once we deny our spouse the blessings of forgiveness the Father reciprocates our ingratitude in kind. For the Father will not bless any home that curses his will. Again in Matthew chapter 6:14 it states, *"For if you forgive people their trespasses (their reckless and willful sins, leaving them, letting them go, and giving up resentment), your heavenly Father will also forgive you. But if you do not forgive others their trespasses (their reckless and willful sins, leaving them letting them go, and giving up resentment), neither will your Father forgive you your trespasses."*

Why then is it easier for outside of the home friends to forgive and love in the Agape sense where it is difficult for couples? Primarily it is because same sexed friends have a leg up on their relationships. It is not because they are compatible by any stretch of the imagination. By definition of their relationship they completely bypass the first category of love being Eros and proceed directly to Philia.

Since most friends are of same sex they don't have to view one another as anything other than friends first. So an outside of the home relationship starts on a higher plane to begin with. It begins on the level of love, communication and forgiveness. This also makes it easier for them to move towards an Agape love, which is only one stage higher than friendship love. The great difficulty of opposite gender relationships is that they start at the lowest level of love.

"Love takes no account of the evil done to it. It does not rejoice at injustice and unrighteousness, but rejoices when right and truth prevail. Love bears up under anything and everything that comes."

1 Corinthians 13:5-7

Don't Let the Sun Go Down on Your Anger

It is far easier to forgive than it is to hold onto a grudge. Most people would believe the opposite to be true but I will show you the error of that thinking. God commanded in Ephesians 4:26 *"Do not let the sun go down while you are still angry."* God the Father knew that not only will your day be destroyed in an anger state but so would your night. In fact, if you went to bed in an anger state there is a good possibility that you would wake up the same come the next morning or possibly for the rest of your life.

The sin of unforgiveness is the most costly and deadliest of all of the sins of the bible. In its roots it is responsible for more internal diseases, wars and murders than anything else on the planet today. It causes you to frown, turning down the corners of your mouth until you achieve permanent lines on your face. If you are a woman, there is not enough makeup or botox to reverse what the act of forgiveness does for frown lines. It causes people to call in sick from work or quit their jobs because they cannot get along with their coworkers. It is the impetus for a family member to cease communication with his entire family for life.

Imagine the savings to your personal medical insurance if we could just learn how to forgive. It has been said that most of us die not from what we eat, but what is eating at us. Imagine the savings of being able to avoid expensive counseling sessions. The medical community would lose billions of dollars annually. I once remember counseling a woman who believed it was impossible for humans to forgive. I encouraged her to read Luke 1:37, *"That for with God nothing is ever impossible and no word from God shall be without power or impossible of fulfillment."* So again if we cannot see our way to doing an act that is kind, just or right, we are acting in our will and not God's will. For humans the biggest tug of war is between doing what God wants when we are happy and doing what we feel when we feel disappointed.

The Satan Syndrome

The Satan Syndrome attacks anyone that harbors unforgiveness, anger or sexual vice within their heart. It is an insidious disease that grows within long before it manifest on the outside. It causes a once beautiful face to contort into a dragon like image. You see, in heaven all of the angels are beautiful, as Lucifer once was, but the angels that rebelled against God were not only expelled but stripped of that beauty. The head rebel, Lucifer, lost his name and became Satan [the devil]. His image was changed to that of a hideous beast that has a body of a dragon. The angels that rebelled with him lost their bright glow for a darkened smoke-like appearance. This reminds me of the verse that asks: if your light has been darkened, how deep does that darkness go?

From half a block away it is usually easy to determine the approach of a facially attractive man or woman. Why? Because the society we live in tends to focus on exterior beauty. This is why one is easily fooled by the appearance of the face when placing their trust in others. The nicer the face, the more the guard becomes lowered. For so long we have believed that the young are more facially appealing than the elderly. But I tell you the reverse is true. It is hard to tell if one is darkened when they are young because they can disguise it with a smile or attractive features.

But when they are aged, their life's journey to honor the light [God] or the domination of darkness [the devil] manifests itself in the downturned appearance of a wrinkled face with frown indentions between the eyes and about the mouth. Then and only then does true inner beauty come out that has been hidden behind protective layering. But the way God sees all humans becomes finally known to humankind through the face. Equally, at the distance of a half block you can tell in the features of an elderly person that beauty has rested within. If they have become decent and loving over time, even wrinkles serve little more than to enhance their outward expression of love. But for the negative person the dragon like appearance of Satan takes over their face and personality.

Learning How to Forgive Your Parents

We have identified that some pains might have come about due to our upbringing. But I'm here to tell you that you can forgive your parents and clear their conscience and yours at the same time. Because a lot of the mistreatment, mistakes and hurt that your parents may have visited upon you was not their original intention for marriage or children. I find myself teaching couples this truth all the time before I can ever counsel them on their own problems. I awaken their senses about the true spirit of their parents. I do this by telling them that no child grows up with the intention of abusing or mistreating their own children.

No parent makes a conscious plan to inflict pain that they could not bear themselves. They went through something painful themselves in their youth that changed their makeup as a loving individual. They believed later on in life, after getting married and having children, that they could keep those pains in check. But that idea is fine on a perfect day without any financial or personal problems. But the difficulty happens when they are under maximum pressure, for that is the same way that the disease was given unto them. Unforgiveness always manifests itself to destroy beautiful environments when people are generally stressed out.

Most of the couples who came to me also had children and I witnessed to the last a mirrored behavior of their upbringing. If the wife received pain as a child she issued it in kind to her child in the present. If a father went through something painful with his parents he put his children through the same. So even though these couples came to see me with complaints about their parents they were blind to the fact that they were doing the same thing to their children. It is true that whatever gets pressed down upon you becomes you unless you are willing to forgive your transgressors. Forgiveness must be given in order to break any painful cycle. Those that can forgive end the cycle of hatred and unforgiveness with this generation of their family.

The Best They Could Myth

Before we can begin to forgive our parents we have to be honest with ourselves. If not, no forgiveness will be long lasting to the person who offers it or to the person who receives it. I am faced with having to tell this to men and women who come to me with the motto that their parents did the best they could. In saying this I understand that they are trying to protect something in their parent's behavior or standards that they did not particularly agree with. The reason the line *the best they could* is a total myth to me is because it always hides something else.

I especially understand that the person who is saying this about their parents has some opinions that they would like to express but they are not doing so. Now in no way do I wish to demonize the parents because, as a parent myself, I know full well how trying it can be to raise children even in the best of circumstances. But truthfully someone who gives their parents' shortcomings absolution through saying it was the best they could do will surely present it to their children when they give them less then they could. That is why once children start to fail in life they announce to their parents that they are doing the best that they can.

As parents and spouses we can always do better, but when we choose not to we present an excuse to cover our shortcomings. In fact, the very same person who insists that they are doing the best at home does spectacular at work for the company that employs them. In most any country on the planet you can find a much higher output on the job then you can find at home by the same parents. For no one calls up a pizza parlor to order the best you can make pizza. No one would tolerate the best you can utilities of water, electric or gas. Who in sound mind would go to a supermarket where they sold the best they could food?

The best my parents could is precisely the reason why people come to counseling mad about something their spouse is or is not doing. This is precisely why I attack this myth to make the person truthful with themselves. But ultimately I need them to be able to forgive their parents as humans — just as God would. If they can successfully do this then they can spend less time being angry at Thanksgiving and holidays together. No one wants to be trapped in a long holiday stay over with a person who is angry about past mistakes. God the Father instructs us all not to let the sun go down on our anger. I take this instruction to heart in my everyday life as if it were gold falling from above. I make a conscious effort to learn what time the sun is going to set each day. Then I make sure that I forgive everyone whom I believed has wronged me during that day.

I also ask the Father for forgiveness for anyone I may have wronged that same day. I also use that time to get rid of any anger or inthoughtsification that I may carry into the night. I pray to the Father to forgive me for getting angry or offending anyone during that day. Before I started doing this I dealt with forgiveness the way most of us do, and that was by not forgiving. Most of us are good at remembering every negative thing that ever happened in our lives but are challenged to recall the good.

When we were told not to let the sun go down on our anger it was *to prevent the devil from gaining a foothold in our lives*. But many of us have let many suns, moons and stars set on our anger. In fact we have allowed decades and generations to pass on this same anger. This is open rebellion to the word of God's laws of love and forgiveness. What good is religion if it does not change the character and save the soul? The only thing that remains is the hollow teachings of the Pharisees who had no genuine love or forgiveness.

The Path to Forgiveness

The whole premise of converting to Christianity from secularism is in essence a death to one's old self or sinful nature. The literal baptism commemorates the death, burial and resurrection of spirit. This is why our greatest strength is in coming to the Father, while our greatest weakness is running away from redemption. I can think of no other way to truly learn how to forgive and rise above past hurt or guilt than for one's old self to die.

I enjoy meeting people wherever I travel or work who have decided to convert to the best in themselves. Recently I met a woman who typifies this process despite having been raised in a background that would sour anyone's outlook on life. You see, Jacqueline grew up in a home where she describes her mother as very cold and distant from her. In fact, she truly believed that her mom preferred her brother over her. For this reason Jacqueline found herself as a young girl growing ever closer to her father. She recounts that her father, in her opinion, never really received unconditional love from his own wife.

By the time she was a teenager her father had developed a drinking problem. She regretfully remembers him joking about how a ditch jumped out in front of him as he was driving. Actually he covered his unsafe behavior behind the wheel by insisting that he could control his drinking habit. But by the time Jacqueline was preparing to go to college the habit had already taken control of him. She says that she does not believe that he would have been able to conquer this deadly habit had it not been for the fact that he developed ulcers from drinking.

As I spoke to Jacqueline I found myself wanting her to see her way to forgive her mother, much as she had learned to overlook her father's indiscretions. In Jacqueline's eyes her father could do little wrong. His behavior exemplified a loving father and provider to her. She remembers how he could fix anything around the house to save the family's income. *"He fixed the family car, the furnace, he even dug up the septic system to make it less costly when the repairmen came out to fix it. But what my mother only noticed were the little things, such as his leaving water droplets on the sink after he washed his hands."* So it came to me as no shock that a young lady without the love of her mother would by early adult life carry on a wayward and promiscuous existence as a cry for attention.

She insists that for awhile as a young adult she was so disenfranchised with her mother that she suggested that her father divorce her for someone who would truly make him happy. Once she walked in on her father as he sat on the edge of his bed crying. She asked him in earnest what was the matter. He confessed to her that he knew that things should be better between them as a family. But even after all of the lack of love that was experienced in the home, she admitted that her father still loved his wife. I told her that it is understandable because he sees something in her that nobody else sees.

What has this upbringing done to Jacqueline's daily life? It has inspired her to see men in a view opposite her mother's. She has been brought to find God, the Father, and attends church as often as she can. She has a very cheerful demeanor and invites people often to her congregation. Against all odds she was even successful at getting her parents to attend her church after many years of staying away in avoidance. I counseled her to continue in the direction she is going. For you see, Jacqueline has gotten off the broad road and is now on the narrow path that leads to God and everlasting life.

What makes me most proud of her is that she is in the process of forming a business that provides romantic settings and dinners for couples who lack experience planning romance. I wish you could see her face light up when she explains to people her mission to bring love to romantically challenged homes.

Learning How to Forgive Everyone Else

If you can learn to forgive your parents and your spouse than it should be a breeze to forgive anyone else — including yourself. Not simply for the sake of forgiving but in the understanding of the human levels of love. The people that offend you currently only operate out of whatever level of love they have achieved thus far, just as you do. This is why the Father judges the heart and not the words or exterior appearances of people. Peter writes in Acts 10:34 that *"Most certainly and thoroughly I now perceive and understand that God shows no partiality and is no respecter of persons."* If someone has not achieved any higher level than Eros love for himself and society it will be a far stretch on your part to expect Agape love from them.

Only the Father knows that the person who hurt you may have been hurt that way by someone else. For the bible tells us that *"Vengeance is mine sayeth the Lord."* His judgments will weigh out the truth of his spirit. But to reduce your level of love to a lower one in order to match the anger of an enemy only secures a place in hell for two people instead of one. What we will be judged upon is that we did not try to bring that person up from a lower love to a higher love.

Learning How to Forgive Yourself

*"The ultimate
test of forgiveness is in
people being able to release
themselves from a painful past that
they had no power over
to control."*

— *Charles Rivers*

More prominent in the minds of people who attend counseling beyond forgiveness of parents is forgiveness of self. A person must be brought to self forgiveness before they can expunge destructive behaviors from their life. Most men and women that I encourage to forgive themselves admitted to me that they did not have a personal problem or that they did not need to forgive themselves. This was completely untrue, for all people are changed by their upbringing and environment. Most people, wives or husbands, that came to me complaining about their mates thought that they had not changed since childhood. They had already issued themselves blanket absolution over their entire lives.

But I showed them that a child starts at one level then receives pains, pornography and the like from the world. This takes their level of love and humanity down a few notches. Therefore they must be brought back up to that level before they feel a sense of resolution over their pains. I once revealed to a woman a sure fire test to see if you approve of who you have become. I told her only one person can stand in judgment of her.

She told me that she knew who judged her behavior. I said, "For sure one day God will stand in judgment of you, but today you will stand in judgment of yourself." I asked her to vividly think back to her earliest memory of younger days: when she had a more innocent demeanor and love for any and everyone.

I told her even at that time she could tell if someone loved or was mean spirited simply by looking at them. The loving person draws little children in with their demeanor and the mean repel them away. In fact, in most children's neighborhoods there is always a house where they determine an older man or woman as the scary person. They avoid this house like the plague because of the person's attitude.

"The enemy within us
is far more dangerous
then the enemy without, for
he knows your every move
before it is made"

— *Charles Rivers*

So I asked her if she was ready to judge herself and her attitude. I told her to imagine for a moment that she could separate the little innocent child she was from the adult she now is. Now if that little child came in this room right now and looked her in the face, what would she think? Would she be glad of what she had become or would she wish for something different? Would she see herself as that scary person on the block that she and her friends tried to avoid? Would she want to rush to her arms to be embraced by love or would she perceive an absence of love? No one can stand in better judgment of our behavior on earth than we can.

Okay I Can Forgive, But How Does One Forget?

I have heard this statement often enough in counseling from topics ranging from adultery to a series of smaller offenses. So many people can recant every negative situation they went through in life but are challenged to remember the good. During our growing years most of us have changed physical addresses many, many times. Our hearts and minds have a tendency to stay stuck in events and situations at those same physical addresses for what we choose not to let go. The bible gives us Jesus Christ as the highest aspiration to forgiveness. This verse makes known human frailties and reveals the struggles involved in becoming Christ-like, but nevertheless, it is a path worth staying on.

In Philippians 3:11-14 we are told *"That if possible I may attain to the (spiritual and moral) resurrection [that lifts me] out from among the dead (even while in the body). Not that I have now attained (this ideal), or have already been made perfect, but I press on to lay hold of and make my own , that for which Christ Jesus has laid hold of me and made me His own. I do not consider, brethren, that I have captured and made it my own (yet): but one thing I do [It is my one aspiration]: forgetting what lies behind and straining forward to what lies ahead, I press on toward the goal to win the [supreme and heavenly] prize to which God in Christ Jesus is calling us upward."*

Freeing Your Home of Sexual Sins and Addictions

*"One cannot volunteer
their free will if it is held
captive by other passions."*

— *Charles Rivers*

There is but one thing in life that stands between you and your ability to volunteer freely of your heart and that is whatever addictive behavior you hold nearer to your heart than your spouse. In Mathew 6:21 we are told, *"For where your treasure is, there your heart will be also."* So in order to grow into a closer bond we will discuss some of the root causes of addictive behavior and how to rid your home of them. We can never freely give of our hearts if our minds are dominated by unforgiveness, hate and immoral behaviors. Without forgiveness the heart grows numb to feelings of true love long before it dies to self.

If what we do for a life beyond work does not ignite our passion for living then we will lean on artificial stimulants for that lost excitement. This is where drugs, alcohol, pornography and the like originate from. When people replace their free time or their zest for life with jobs and responsibilities they open the door wide to all sorts of negative coping crutches known as addictions. Addictive habits have the tendency to initially feel like they help us cope with all sorts of things we refuse to face up to. Addictions are our way of dealing with the mundane stresses of life. But with each use of the addiction our threshold of things we have the ability to cope with becomes lowered. Besides that, addictions will ultimately take more from your life then they will ever add to it.

The Birth of Some Adulthood Addictions

Some of the addictions we use to cope today originated from past stuff we refuse to address as far back as infancy. Infants and little children have to be satisfied immediately to balance their moods. We continue this during our growing years to adulthood where we try to maintain an unrealistic existence. We strive to prevent anything bad from befalling our lives.

But this is not possible, for even God himself challenges us to go higher while standing beside us through life's many ups and downs.

Addictions May Vary by Gender and Character Type

Men and women react differently under situations of boredom and stress. While boredom may trigger some addictions in women, stress is more of an addictive indicator in the lives of men. Men and women both exist within normal boundaries on our personal morale scale until we go through an internal or external crisis. Beyond this point we consciously choose to leave that morale scale to use addictions in hopes of centering ourselves. The addictive person does not center his/herself in the Lord but in his/her own scales of balance. The addictive person operates in the mind and with their own resources to deal with pain. In essence, we become doctor and pharmacist in the management of pain and pleasure.

Some men who procrastinate to a level of risk in their jobs, homes or personal lives may reach for alcohol or sexual deviancies. When procrastination leads to stress and an addictive nature, this is usually our green light to act on that event or project we have been putting off. For some people that would mean working on a failing relationship or for others moving beyond a career that robs their soul. But the answer for most should be a calling to move closer to the Father for the comfort we seek.

External Addictions Verses Internal Addictions

Of all of the addictions to have, I believe pornography is the worst. Here's why: most of the addictions we normally face have to be placed within our bodies before we can become addicted. Sure enough, we have the ability to receive lifelong addictions through any one of our five senses. But the worst addictive nature to take internally comes through the eyes, the lamp of the body. We are told in Luke 11:34-36 that, *"Your eye is the lamp of your body. When your eyes are good, your whole body also is full of light. But when they are bad, your body also is full of darkness. See to it, then, that the light within you is not darkness. Therefore, if your whole body is full of light, and no part of it dark, it will be completely lighted, as when the light of a lamp shines on you."*

The Fastest Acting Addiction is Neither Ingested nor Inhaled

*"An addiction
is forever thwarted
once its captive begins to come to
grips with its causes instead
of managing its
symptoms."*

— Charles Rivers

All humans are born with what will be their future sexuality. Now here is where we get in trouble. Everyone has that young friend who somehow magically finds a pornographic book that he /she wants to share with you. Others have those dirty little relatives that unintentionally leave us easy access to pornographic films and books. Now once you view these items with your eyes they go straight to your very soul. You are now hooked, but differently than any other addiction. If you were not addicted to anything and I placed a pack of cigarettes on a table beside a bottle of beer and a pornographic book something interesting would reveal itself within a human psyche.

Simply viewing the cigarettes on that table will not get you hooked on them. You would have to inhale the smoke into your body before they would have any effect on the pleasure centers of your brain. Then you would have to get beyond the distaste and the gag effect before their addictive nature could ever take a hold and dominate your free will. Similarly, by viewing the beer you would not get drunk or addicted. You would have to drink many cans, depending on your threshold or tolerance of addiction to it. Then you would have to get beyond its unpleasant taste before the addiction formed to control your free will. But to open the pornographic book and view something you know nothing of has the potential to get you hooked inquisitively on one page. It arouses you and makes you desire more. Like any other addiction, it will make you lie about the fact that you engage in it.

With pornography a person neither has to face the gag effect nor get beyond the distaste. The only distaste barrier to be defeated is our morale scale. Once you take in the pornographic material with the eyes, the brain becomes addicted and your lamp becomes darkened.

From that day forward your views of the opposite gender become skewed in your eyes to fulfill a natural high. Your light upon viewing pornography will be permanently snuffed out. When it comes to viewing the opposite gender, one must now rely on the other four senses to understand true love. One is promised that their eyes will be opened at a young age after viewing pornography, but actually his eyes are closed and he forever thinks filthily of himself where his thoughts were once pure.

A spouse who has relied upon pornography to darken his soul must now learn how to listen to his spouse. He must learn how to touch his spouse with his hands in a non-sexual way. He must learn how to taste his spouse with a gentle kiss. He must learn how to enjoy his spouse's smell outside of a completely sexual perfumed state. An addiction will steal what is left of your pride before taking its final hold of you. The nature of an addiction is that just before it consumes the life of its participants it has them pass it on to another who is addiction-free. With porn, you don't inhale it, you don't inject it — you just view it.

*"Most modern
addictions are driven by
the advertisers' futile need to profit
from the addictive nature of
his customers' five
senses."*

— *Charles Rivers*

I was asked recently what I attribute the breakdown of the modern family to. Would it be a sexually focused society and the ease of attaining adult materials in stores and the internet? Actually the person who asked me this was half right and didn't even know it. The breakdown of the modern family patterns itself after a nation that turned its back on God for sexual liberties. But more evident is a nation to which has reduced itself to an Erotic type of love climate in which they cannot rise to Philia or Agape. For an Erotic type of love is the death of any relationship hoping for longevity. Erotic love is such that someone could freely share their body with a stranger they would surely deny their heart, mind and spirit to.

Why the Strong Hold of Pornography and Extramarital Affairs?

*"Most people turn
to Erotic love because it
is one of the last loves they are sure to
feel in areas of life where human
touch becomes void of Philia
and Agape love."*

— *Charles Rivers*

In Matthew 12:29 we are asked this question: *"How can a person go into a strong man's house and carry off his goods without first binding the strong man? Then indeed he may plunder the house."* This bible verse gives us the analogy of how even the strongest among us spiritually can be bound by what we have as a weakness. The will to resist addictive behaviors must be hijacked before people can be bound and led in a destructive direction willfully.

No drug has any control over our bodies without us first submitting our free will to it. In fact, once people escape addictions, they choose to take back the free will they allowed the drugs to control. Drugs have no hold over the body except that they have the key to sabotaging the body's own chemistry. In the brain the chemical dopamine and serotonin helps to regulate our moods and well being. The chemical dopamine helps to transmit nerve impulses within the brain between sending and receiving nerve receptors. Serotonin is widely distributed through the body and the brain and affects change on our emotional moods.

Cocaine and other drugs hijack the body's natural production of the chemical known as dopamine, thereby blocking its steady flow between neuron connectors. It blocks one side of the receiving connectors so that dopamine is able to build up on one side, raising it to a level of euphoria. In a sense we are not high on the drugs we take but on our own body's chemistry. The chemical dopamine is released at a proportionately higher rate during sex, equivalent to an intense drug high for just a brief moment during orgasm.

Dopamine is also released at a constantly higher rate while you're watching pornographic material than in your normal lovemaking. This is why no one should accept the advice of any therapist on television or in person who tells you that adult films will enhance your lovemaking. The only thing that will happen is that you will be hooked on the pornography and not a healthy sex life with your spouse. The same goes for marriages with people who are serial adulterers or fornicators. They end up getting hooked on the dopamenic high in the brain while participating in illicit sexual acts more than they do having sex with the person they are with.

Don't Allow Secular Sexuality to Sneak into Your Christian Home

When Christian couples come to me with marriage problems, I often find a secular influence has been infecting their sexual life as a couple. Either the husband or the wife that is supposed to be walking in the ways of Christ will profess that they are in the "dog house." This is a terminology used when one spouse denies the other sexual love to punish them for a perceived wrong. Either husband or wife may be taking up residence on the couch or in some other part of the house even though they should be sleeping together.

This behavior is most dangerous to the life of any committed relationship. It is dangerous because one spouse creates a glass ceiling for the other in one of the three areas of God's love. Usually when you do this in a society that is obsessed with Erotic love someone will come along to break that glass ceiling. Strange people beyond the borders of your home, who have the intention of committing adultery, target your spouse in this vulnerable state.

But the reason all illicit relationships, pornography and fantasies fail to deliver satisfied love over the long haul is that your concentration is never on the person you are engaging in a sexual relationship with but the arousal behind it. When you bring only your mind to bed you leave Philia and Agape love at the bedroom door. All you have left is an erotically exciting sexual experience, and this experience is not much different than bringing yourself to orgasm.

The sexual relationship becomes all about you having sex with yourself and your internal thoughts. This is love in the demonic realm.

For one to enjoy love with another in a room they must think of another who is not in the room. The act of sexual love should be with the person you are with and not in your head with your thoughts. Any type of addiction is meant to satisfy the selfish needs of the individual to escape pain for pleasure. Another person engaging in an addiction with you does not receive your pleasure. All the alcohol I can consume will never make my spouse drunk.

That is precisely why a secular erotic-type dating relationship is usually highest touted but shortest lived of any of the three loves. The relationship is mainly sex and the person you are having sex with becomes a tool for your sexual gratification. They are never allowed to rise up to the level of a human, which starts at the Philia level. Most sexually-based relationships refuse to go to this level because they fear this will kill the pleasurable experience of the sexual relationship. It is best that both participants in this natural brain high remain neutral with their feelings and concerns in life in order to protect the great sexual feelings that are aroused by addictive highs.

What these relationships fail to understand is that sex becomes more intimate if you bring all three loves to bed with you. Eros love is fine as a good inducer of the sexual act but it does not honor the openness of the Philia love as in respect to the sexual act. Couples that have a good friendship relationship can communicate their sexual desires towards one another much more easily instead of patterning the sexual acts of adult films. Eros love alone can never understand that couples who exist on an Agape level of love would not want to commit adultery against their spouse. People who have truly achieved Agape love understand that the people who they love should be respected as a creation of God and not as a created pleasure tool.

In teaching couples, I have been known to take from them the tools of using sex as a weapon in the relationship in order to get what they want. For who could withhold water (a metaphor for sex) in a town that is satiated with faucets? In other words, you live in a society where not only will people want to commit adultery with your spouse but it bothers the heck out of them in some sick way to see them thirst for something that everyone freely offers.

Create More Sunny Days than Rainy

*"Change your
thoughts and you change
the world."*

— Norman Vincent Peale

The late Reverend Norman Vincent Peale once said, *"Change your thoughts and you change the world."* What the Reverend meant when he penned this statement many years ago was that if you changed your thoughts of the world from negative to positive, your outlook on everything and everyone around you would follow suit. The physical world that used to frustrate you would not change, but you would — and that is half the battle most of us face in trying times.

Difficult experiences in life have the tendency to bring out the worst in us and, for some of us, depression. We lash out at those we love. This is why if any marriage is to be real and lasting, it is impossible to be strong and one in marriage under trying circumstances in an Eros relationship. You must be at least a Philia relationship, optimally an Agape one. Christian couples who are not friends in hard times usually fall apart over the incident and pull apart from one another. In troubled times, an "everyone for themselves" attitude will exist in these homes.

But these are the times when we should never bolt to decisions. Between the flight or fight mentality there is always room for pause. If you could do well under trying times as a single person, then with your spouse at your side things should be twice as nice. If the bad times that we all face bring out the blaming mechanism in you, then this is another reason to use the time to improve yourself. Remember we learn more about ourselves with someone of the opposite nature then we ever could in the presence of someone of like mind.

As a couple, you are not the first people to go through ups and downs. In Deuteronomy 8:11-17, God had a message for the Israelites who believed themselves once up and then brought low. The Father is asking of us in good times and bad to stand on our belief in Him and who we are as Christians.

The Israelites were told, *"Beware that you do not forget the Lord your God by not keeping His commandments, His precepts, and His statutes which I command you today, Lest when you have eaten and are full, and have built godly houses and live in them, And when your herds and flocks multiply and your silver and gold is multiplied and all you have is multiplied, Then your [minds and] hearts be lifted up and you forget the Lord your God, Who brought you out of the land of Egypt, out of the house of bondage, Who led you through the great and terrible wilderness, with its fiery serpents and scorpions and thirsty ground where there was no water, but Who brought you forth water out of the flinty rock,*

Who fed you in the wilderness with manna, which your fathers did not know, that He might humble you and test you, to do you good in the end. And beware lest you say in your [mind and] heart, My power and the might of my hand have gotten me this wealth. But you shall [earnestly] remember the Lord your God, for it is He who gives you power to get wealth, which He may establish His covenant which He swore to your fathers, as it is this day."

Every occasion of financial loss, tragedy or trauma in our lives is not at the hands of the Father. But it is also said *"that the Lord giveth and it is the Lord that taketh away."* If we are supposed to learn something in life but have insulated ourselves from life with money or people, then that is precisely what we will be liberated from to get our attention. In fact, I have seen one vein that runs throughout this promise. If God the Father withdraws funds from us then he will do the same for everyone around you that you would run to for security.

Once we have learned the lesson we are supposed to learn, our wealth will be returned and often times in spades. At the same time he will give prosperity to those around you who have stood faithfully beside us despite the difficulty. So if the Father should have to get your attention in these ways, seek to learn the lesson with all deliberate speed. If you ask several friends and family members to help, all of sudden they will find themselves without, so just be patient and understand that God is at work in your marriage.

Often times without knowing it, people interfere when God trying to get a particular person's attention. Just as fast as God closes doors in front of someone, another person tries to run ahead of Him and prop them open.

They seek to do this with money, advice or assistance. When we do this we risk being removed from the lesson the Father is wishing another to learn. But often a relationship's financial undoing comes at our own hands. In our heads we carry a picture of what we want as an ultimate goal. We see the finish line just as the marathoner would at the beginning of the race. But we are not qualified to win the race because we are better suited for sprinting than running long distance.

When times get rough, as they often do, we refuse to acknowledge them in our grandiose plans for success. Every runner does not win the race the first time out of the gate. Success in any circle of life comes with an equal measure of trials and tribulations. The down times are what shape the winner. He or she does not view unplanned events as the end but as a hurdle to be overcome.

Children are Born Conquerors

We start off life by learning to crawl and then to stand, only to fall and get back up again. Ultimately we learn to run at speeds incomprehensible to our infant brains. The same is true with God, depending on if you are a baby Christian or whether you have learned to place upon you the full armor of God. As children, we are invincible; we compete in a contest to win, avoiding, at all cost, the loss factor.

Then somewhere along the way we try to isolate and insulate ourselves from anything going wrong in our lives. Some of us do it financially and others by planning so far in advance that our lives would run out before our security network would. We can make avoidance of pain such a priority that the natural pleasures of life slip past.

Don't Let the Down Times Make You Turn Inward

Pain has a way of making all of us withdraw and turn inward. Sometimes we go through times that are particularly trying, so much so that a vacuous hole in your faith opens up that may send you back to the crutches you depended on in your secular life. We begin to doubt God as we become lead attendants at our self-designed pity party. If you are married and do this, what happens to your spouse? It becomes possible for them to be left alone and out of the loop while in your presence. When we are at our lowest is the best time to give outward, remembering first that all charity should begin at home. So before we start to assist strangers we should do something for our spouses that they desire out of our love for them.

Remember I said *desired* not *need*, for there is time each day for those types of request. But there is no better time than the present to give to others what you need the most now. For if you are in pain you are experiencing the gift of feeling what others may feel on a constant basis. This makes us more human when we can reach out and understand another's pains instead of writing them a card to cover ourselves.

But for God's sake, whatever you do, get out of your own head and away from inthoughtsification. What can you do today for someone in your time of need? Whatever that may be, ensure you bring your spirits up through doing it. Being down and downing others has never been a motivating factor in the lives of people.

In Proverbs 28:14 we are cautioned to this when it says, *"Blessed (happy, fortunate, and to be envied) is the man who reverently and to be envied) is the man who reverently and worshiply fears (the Lord) at all times (regardless of circumstances), but who hardens his heart will fall into calamity. Like a roaring lion or a ravenous and charging bear is a wicked ruler over a poor people."*

Celebrating the Bad Times as Good

I have always suggested this to couples and I use this exercise myself. You may think its crazy, but it gets even wilder. Go to your grocer's pastry section and purchase a sheet cake with stenciling of whatever hurdle you are facing in life currently. For example, stenciling like "we are broke and we can only go up from here". What about putting the amount in dollars of the debt you currently owe to your creditors.

"If one's intrinsic value is based solely upon earnings potential, it is a safe bet to assume that his or her internal emotions will be guided by the up and downward ticks of the national economy."

— Charles Rivers

Get either a bottle of non-alcoholic or regular champagne and commemorate the moment, for, with God, you won't be there long. If we don't celebrate the bad times in life, we are not celebrating life. For life entails the good, bad and indifferent. If we live only to celebrate the good times, they may become few and far between. The good times in life are sometimes sprinkled between the lulls and trials. It makes it much easier to come back from a hit in life if you don't begrudge yourself through it.

I've given you the medicine to allow you to look back and laugh at the experience. Remember that you can never have any memorable occasions without film, so take plenty of pictures. This is written poetically well in the Psalms 30:5, *"Sing to the Lord O you saints of His, and give thanks at the remembrance of His holy name. For His anger is but for a moment but His favor is life. Weeping may endure for a night, but joy comes in the morning."*

Now that you have come to grips with your problems as a couple and changed your outlook on the situation, prepare to receive increase. For the Lord our heavenly Father rewards learning. So receive wholeheartedly the lesson in the down times and prepare for the success that will ultimately come during the good.

*Evolve
into one
beautiful couple, for you
dared to risk your heart with
someone who was separate and distinct
from your will. You have successfully died to self
if you have strived in earnest to live God's
Agape love. Along the journey you
have become a more likeable,
loveable and easy to
live with human
being.*

Book 4

LEAVE
OBSERVE
VOLUNTEER
EVOLVE

*"For what
activates the best
in all of us does not reside
within any of us, but rest in those
we allow to influence
our soul."*

— *Charles Rivers*

The Evolution of the Human Spirit in Spirit

*"But the fruit
of the Spirit is love, joy,
peace, patience, kindness,
goodness, faithfulness,
gentleness and
self control."*

— *Galatians 5:22-23*

Throughout history many people have asked what beauty could ever come from such cruel tragedies of the world we live in. My answer to that question is that there is much more to be learned and healed over tragedy then there ever will be in the good times. Jesus Christ endured great suffering and pains as he bore each lash of the soldier's whip for all of the sins of mankind. Even under tremendous pains of being nailed to the cross, he could already see triumph for Christians through the tragedy of the moment. After the third day, he ascended to the right hand of his father in heaven and opened the door to salvation and the most beautiful religion that ever graced the face of God's green earth.

There are far too many stories and examples of people who have either turned their lives or other people's lives around because of pain or tragedy. I am reminded of just such an example that proves this type of evolution of the human spirit. It is the story of a little girl called Denise. Denise, as a young adult, was frequently overheard saying, *"I have no talent. What can I do in life?"* She had allowed a damaged past to color her opinion of her self worth and her importance in this world. Denise was born into poverty in the rural Southern portion of the state of Texas. By the age of six months, she was in the care of her cousins as foster parents. She was second to the youngest of six other siblings who had been forcibly removed from the care of her birth parents by the local authorities.

The local authorities would charge of the parents with abuse. Denise would never again come to live under the same roof with her natural parents. Denise did find a good foster home and had come to accept her new foster mother as a loving person. Unfortunately Denise's care giver died while she was thirteen years of age. This was devastating to the emotions of a girl who had never seen any sense of permanence in her young life. Her attitude about life took on a defensive posture, which is what one expects from a child who becomes skeptical of attachments to people who are transient in their lives.

Due to her foster mother's passing, she never really recovered her drive for excelling in school. By the age of seventeen years she became disenfranchised with the public school system and decided to drop out of high school. By the age nineteen years she decided to marry the man she fell in love with. It did not take long for the fallout of that painful type of upbringing to threaten the safety of her blossoming marriage. But her husband, knowing similar pains from his own upbringing, decided to stick it out with Denise for as long as it took for her to heal. Their relationship became whole after her husband educated himself in the trials, pains and joys that were similar to all marriages.

That was almost ten years ago, and that young lady who was healed and saved is my wife. She has been the inspiration for all five books that I have ever written on marriage and relationships. She is the reason that I committed to instructing couples in love at the seminars we hold. If not for her past tragedy, you would not be able to experience the triumph of healing your relationship through this book you are reading.

She had been mistaken many years ago when she believed she had no gift to give to the world. Because God wanted us to partner together, great things have happened to heal both of our lives: past and present. Because of that little girl, my books are read by thousands of people each year who have experienced marital pains. So everyone who needed help would receive it. We have donated thousands of books free of charge to libraries all across America. I believe there is a little Denise in every town all around the world who thinks of themselves just the way she did. Yes that small girl from little Southern town has been God's greatest tool for relationship change.

For I have learned that what was best in me did not reside in me, but lived in her most secretive unhealed areas. Most likely the same applies in your Christian home. A mother, who has a son who graduated at the top of his class as an architect, spoke to me a month ago. The mother revealed to me that she doesn't know where her child received that gift because she struggles to draw stick men on paper. There are timeless stories to where either because of birth, marriage tragedy or encouragement people have risen to the occasion and created something great where there was absence of will.

Keep Your Heart Open to Change

"God has given us
two ears and one mouth,
so we have to do twice as much
listening as we do speaking."

— *Les Brown*

As Christian couples we must try to learn from one another instead of just teaching and preaching. For if two people are to successfully communicate it will have to exist on a two way street. When we talk at our spouse, this is known as dictating and not communication. Communication is the exchange of information or ideas. But often we get stuck in an immature rut of toning out one another unless it serves our greater good.

If we don't allow input in from a shared coupling then there can be no relationship. It only falls apart from the weight of its own indifference. At this point, if the couple does not rectify the situation, they will both seek relationships outside of the home. It may be from the opposite gender for sex or the same gender for friendship. Because all of us, at sometime in our lives, need someone to communicate with. That is why most people talk their friends' ears off — because they cannot communicate effectively with their own spouse.

*"A person will
sabotage their individual
happiness when they cease
to feel importance in
their daily life."*

— *Charles Rivers*

A married man who cannot communicate with his wife finds his way into topless nightclubs where women reveal their bodies while people who don't like themselves or their spouses much look on. A wife who finds herself in the same loveless relationship discovers that she has grown a fondness for a coworker who sees her as her husband once did.

Her coworker will find no problem with acting on the opportunity to ensnare a wife who is in pain for his own erotic gratification. When we engage in these relationships we don't move forward but backwards into the realm of the Erotic love.

*"When you're
green you're growing,
and when you stop you
start to rot."*

— *Ray Krok*

Mr. Krok, the founder of the McDonalds restaurant corporation, was right when he made this true statement concerning business. He gave us the analogy of any plant that grows from seed to bloom has a green life cycle until its preset maturity date. Then the plant starts to slowly die and then to rot. We can also make this comparison to relationships that start out on fire only to end with a fizzle. In marriage, you have to come up with just as many ideas as you would lend your business to make it extremely successful.

There is not a business in the world that if successful did not gage where they were and how they could be more profitable and productive in the upcoming year. The point we refuse to grow with our spouse will be remembered as our relationship's maturity date. Some relationships are fast growing weeds and others are slow growing oaks. In the marriage relationship the Lord gives us a lot of small instances in which to practice being receptive to our spouse's input.

One spouse prefers to go to a fast food restaurant while the other wants to go to a finer restaurant. One likes canned green beans and the other can't stand them. She parks in the driveway while he prefers the street. These small times of flexibility are merely child's play for the larger decisions that lie ahead. If, as a couple, you cannot stay open to an agreement for the small things, you will absolutely crash over the decisions concerning bankruptcy, death and out of state career changes.

Why the Agreement of Two Over the One?

It is the better decision made by two instead of one. It is better to live as two instead of one. In Ecclesiastes 4:8-11 we are told, *"Here is one alone — no one with him; he neither has child nor brother. Yet there is no end to all his labor, neither does he ask, for whom do I labor and deprive myself good? This is also vanity (emptiness, falsity, and futility); yes, it is a painful effort and an unhappy business. Two are better than one, because they have a good (more satisfying) reward for their labor; For if they fall, the one will lift up his fellow, But woe to him who is alone when he falls and has not another to lift him up! Again, if two lie down together, then they have warmth; but how can one be warm alone?"*

God Intended Marriage to be the World's Most Powerful Team

"Any house
divided against itself
shall not stand."

— Matthew 12:25

We are given many chances to merge opinions and decisions as a practice to draw us nearer to one another. As a treasure and consequence of each agreed upon decision, we are drawn closer to God. Each disagreement and argument draws us ever closer to the devil and destruction. We are not to fight one another but to find agreement from conflict. Have you ever seen a member of a professional football team tackle one of his own players during a game? Teamwork is the basis for all intimate relationships. In our mutual struggle we become bonded with one another towards our goals.

So if you notice a problem in your relationship with unspoken signals, don't wait for the emergency — move with a sense of urgency. Sometimes the human spirit can get so wounded that we won't be able to open up to those closest to us. I see this all the time from couples who fail to recognize non-verbal cues from their spouse that their friends can see from half a mile away. Usually in defense of their actions, a husband or wife will tell me that their spouse should tell them what is wrong. "Do they expect me to be a mind reader?" I am asked. I would settle for this excuse if they had not been so well attuned to reading their out of the home best friend's thoughts.

How Easily are Signals Misread

"For one
can never really give
away a love they are too
frightened to possess
themselves.

— Charles Rivers

"Keith is so lazy he doesn't even help me change his own daughter's diapers," was the condemnation Tammy levied against her husband. Keith and Tammy were the last to visit me at a late night relationship session. Often times couples who come to me are total strangers to marital assistance and lose their ability to speak shortly after sitting down. The next thing they do is usually blame one another with every fiber of their being. But I like to set the tone of the meeting by opening up to the true problems of the relationship instead of going around in circles.

I accomplish this by choosing the spouse who is less boisterous to speak shortly after calming down the louder one. So once I got Tammy calm enough, I told her, that Keith, her husband, was going to tell her something that he has never told her before in his life. I do this because I have discovered that no matter what spirit a marriage is in, spouses hold painful secrets closest to their heart if the other spouse is not open to unblemished intimacy. Tammy sat there with an attitude of believing she knew all there was to know about Keith. All at once he turned towards Tammy and blurted out the unvarnished truth. "I was molested as a child by my Aunt and my sisters."

This childhood trauma was very emasculating for Keith at an age when his sexuality was yet to be formed. This happening in Keith's life gave clear justification as to why, in his mind, he was avoiding changing his daughter's diapers. It was not due to him being lazy but he thought if he could avoid close contact with his daughter in intimate places she would be safe from what happened to him as a child. For so many years Keith had truly thought that whatever was pressed down upon him became him and was just waiting to get out monstrously. I tell you that couple grew closer that afternoon than they ever did over the previous nine years of marriage. Today Keith takes his concerns to God at church to handle instead of trying to bear them on his own.

For you see, the only danger his daughter was in was having a father that was growing ever-so-distant with his love. Since he had never been given any true Agape love at home, he could only offer Erotic love until he became healed. If that child had gotten any older she would have believed her daddy hated her. Also, since he would have been unavailable for love, the doors would be left wide open for young boys to bring pretentious love to her in the form of sex.

Be in Relationship One to Another

"What brought
You through the last ten
years of your life won't carry
you the next ten."

— John Young Phelps

As we come ever closer to the end of this book on love I want you to remember that for every dead end your relationship faces you are being called up higher. If you want to truly call down the awesome power of the God of this universe then you must learn the properties of the mightiest word in the Jewish Torah. The word *Devekut*, pronounced *De·ve·kut* is interpreted in the English language as *Cleave*. In the book Observe, I explained to you the meaning of cleave but we must view its definition as a lifestyle.

There are only two instances in which this word is spoken in relationship between the closeness of two separate entities. If you are reading this book right now you are in the most powerful company. For God the Father shares his style of sacred relationship with man only through its meaning. The first time the word cleave is ever used in the presence of man is in the Garden of Eden in relation to the marriage of Adam and Eve.

The second time it is mentioned in faithful covenant relationship is between almighty God and those who wish to remain closest to him. In Deuteronomy 11:22 God tells us, *"That for if you diligently keep all this commandment which I command you to do, to love the Lord your God, to walk in all His ways, and to cleave to Him."* Then God says he will give you the desires of your heart. Now is that not the same ingredient to getting the desires of your heart in marriage?

When we fail to do this properly, we get ourselves in trouble. Many of us go to church and try to cleave to God in our own way while not cleaving successfully to our own spouses. The Creator shows us that we should cleave in both relationships in order to find out what real love is. When we strive to love him while failing to get along with our spouses we mock the teachings of the Father and the Son. So we must be in relationship with our spouse as we are to God or we pay lip service of our love to both and as a consequence end up not being respected by either.

Learn to Take Corrective Criticism

Disagreements within a marriage represent the checks and balances that the Father placed to bring the relationship to a consensus. A husband represents a wife's consciousness of masculinity and discipline. A wife represents a husband's consciousness to femininity and mercy. It is important to give other than constant negatives that are common to your spouse's own conscious and unconscious thoughts. A friend outside of the body gives credence to all of the positive thoughts and conscious behaviors. This is exactly why people lean more towards a friendship relationship before they do any other when they want to make a decision that impacts their lives.

You can only give positive reflections of your spouse's conscious thoughts if you are in constant relationship with them. Webster's defines the word "relationship" as *a connection, association or involvement, a connection between persons by blood or marriage; kinship.* So if we desire the gift of reciprocal love from God and our spouse we must be in constant relationship in order to cleave. The second greatest thing in cleaving to the Lord is that no matter if you are sick, rich or poor, whatever may come your way, God will be there by your side.

In Hebrews 13:5 says that, *"He (God) Himself has said I will not in any way fail you nor give up nor leave you without support. I will not, I will not, I will not in any degree leave you helpless nor forsake nor let you down."* Now wouldn't it be absolutely fantastic, as husbands and wives, if we could treat our spouses to the same love that God treats us to? We should never forsake our spouses since we are governed by the same principles of cleaving relationships.

Coming Full Circle

*"Life is a process
of discovering oneself. Once
found you are truly lost
and God is at work
within you."*

— *Charles Rivers*

A child is born with a form of Agape love and before that child dies it will have lost and hopefully rediscovered that love to make it to the kingdom of heaven. This is why Jesus Christ proclaimed in Matthew 18:3, *"No one will make it to the kingdom of heaven until they first become as little children again."*

It was as infants that we loved all people regardless of gender and backgrounds. It was as a child that we shared for the sake of sharing. It was as a child that we forgave merely for the sake of forgiveness. Then towards our weaning youth we slowly transition away from Agape love towards Philia love for the people we call our friends. In this stage of life we take on a form of prejudice of not liking people who are not in our group or who don't think as we do. In this stage of our lives, sharing and forgiveness becomes limited to our personal friends only.

Beyond our preteen years, if we are not careful, we transition to the lowest stage of love for the opposite gender. Oddly enough, though our attractions for the opposite gender are the highest they will ever be, our respect for them personally may be the lowest. We may have avoided them our entire young lives but now we are raging with hormones that prepare our bodies for procreation. By this time we are either estranged from God's love or trying to find him in the rush of everyday life. Finding our way back to him will be made easier as a married person then it ever will be single.

After the wedding we are joined in an Eros love relationship, but we can move to a Philia love with our spouse on our return path back to the Father and Agape love. That is why the longest road any one of us will ever take in life is back to finding ourselves and God's love.

Most of our arguments in marriage occur when we are in an Eros relationship with one another — no matter how long we've been married. Some Christian couples carry secular gender wars that should stay beyond their door right into the love of their sanctified homes.

But competition between the couple robs them of closeness and financial support that only a couple could provide for one another. A wife who works and becomes pregnant should be able to count on her husband when she has to take a sabbatical from her job. You cannot count on this type of financial support from a friend. Sure a friend can loan you money and support when you are in a pinch, but can they do it without complaint everyday for the rest of your life?

A husband who is injured and bed bound for a time can count on his wife's income to see him through to wellness. But would you be able to get a friend to do that for five years? When we compete with our spouse it makes about as much sense as two people rowing in a canoe in opposite directions while still expecting to go forward. To do this would cause the canoe to remain in place, spinning in circles. This is the exact image of a marriage where the participants drift into a tailspin. So take the time to know each other beyond the surface. The bible tells us in Mark 12:25 that, *"For when they shall rise from the dead, they neither marry, nor are given in marriage; but are as the angels which are in heaven."* So our earthly relationships represent the only time we will share this type of exclusive love with one another.

Use each and every day to work towards Agape love and to cleave to your spouse. Nowhere in the bible does it suggest that we should cleave to our outside of the home friends or jobs, but we do. In fact we will even let our families go and fight for our friends and jobs. Most families in the technological age can easily service between six hundred to one thousand people a day effectively through schools and jobs. Simultaneously, this same family could fail at servicing just the handful of people that reside within the walls of their Christian homes.

Marriage's Effect on Children and Children's Effect on Marriage

Most children are born to couples when we are still primarily in an Eros relationship. Therefore each child is charged to grow with the marriage for the good or the bad. It would be great if we could begin our relationships at the minimum of the friendship level, but more than likely it is in Eros.

Here is why: we have every intention of finding the right one to be a great spouse, a good parent to our future children. But when we run into someone we deem as attractive we begin an erotic type love with all of our forethought packaged up and thrown to one side until we come off of cloud nine. So if a child is born to us when we are in a stage of arguing and fighting with one another, this becomes their view of the world of love between the opposite genders. Had we had an offspring in the Philia mode of love that child would discover that we talk through our problems. In an Agape mode maybe those same problems wouldn't even concern us.

If You Love the Father, He Will Love the Child

"Many parents see their
children's wants as needs and
their spouse's needs
as wants."

— *Charles Rivers*

Amy sat quietly angry with her arms crossed in a defensive posture at a session between her and her husband. There were several things in their relationship that also disturbed her husband about Amy. Chief on Amy's list of grievances was that her husband never spent as much time with the children as she thought a father should. After gathering enough pertinent information from both sides I concluded that Amy had put her love to her husband, who preceded her beautiful children, on the back burner. Amy had made herself ready to dedicate the rest of her life to her children indifferent to her husband. Sure enough, men should participate in the lives of their children: especially in ways other than being a provider and a disciplinarian. But there is a dilemma in the way men and women see the role of husband.

Males do not go through the birthing process; they don't go through a single ounce of internal growing pains. But most of all they don't have the desire that predates adolescence, as women do, to have children. But what men are great at is being overly protective and guarding of their relationship with their wives if they must share her with anyone else. So wives, if this is your dilemma at home, let me tell you what to do. First, do not pull away from your spouse during pregnancy and especially after delivery. For most adulterous affairs are committed by men of pregnant wives in the first and final trimester of pregnancy.

Why? Because the husbands feel alone in the presence of their wives. A pregnant woman draws her focus inward or towards her friends for support during these critical stages of pregnancy. To the male, an outside observer, the relationship becomes more about the mother and baby and less about the person who helped to create the little one. To bring this husband into the fold all you have to do is show him strong love. Men develop a disconnection after labor with a child if the mother disconnects with them.

So if your love for your husband is not any different than it is for the child, he will love the child. Men see their own small children as an extension of the mother before they will ever truly see them as their children. So if you either hate or neglect the father he will more than likely hate or neglect the child. Now, later on down the road, fathers grow to their rightful position of love for the child and participation with their children if the family remains a unit. But for this man to arrive where he must with his children, he will need your help.

Amy understood this during our session when out of the blue she said, "I see what you're saying, Mr. Rivers. I have been selfish with my love for my children, while at the same time missing what my husband had been lacking." To her husband she replied, "I had massaged our children's feet but I had never massaged your feet and for years I had ignored the pain in yours." This couple is now on the right road, and they are going to make it with God's help.

Ephesians 3:17-19 talks about the true love of Christ possessing one so that they may give it away to another. Chapter 17 says, "*That Christ may dwell in your hearts by faith; that ye, being rooted and grounded in love, May be able to comprehend with all saints what is the breadth, and length, and depth, and height; And to know the love of Christ, which passeth knowledge, that ye might be filled with all the fullness of God.*"

"Love is ever ready to believe the best of every person, its hopes are fadeless under all circumstances, and it endures everything without weakening. Love never fails or becomes obsolete or comes to an end."

1 Corinthians 13:7–8

Every Child is an Individual Creation

*"Children grow
by who we are, more
than what we say or do when
we think they are
watching."*

— *Charles Rivers*

It is a safe bet to say that by the time our children attend the first grade a part of their character are already set in cement. As parents, we must avoid the temptation to paint them with the same brush that society uses on them. This is done primarily in the home or out of it by the labels we place on them. If your child is a boy, you could fear him getting in trouble, hanging around with the wrong influences. If we have a daughter we could fear other children offering her drugs, her getting pregnant, or something worse. Most parents have these fears long before their children even reach school age.

When we do this we send our children the message: I expect the worst of you. It is shortly after this that we find ourselves not let down by their behaviors. Replace this outlook with a positive one in the future. We cannot be Christians and believers in God while being disbelievers in his most precious of creations. To view your child as an outcome instead of a person is contradictory to the way you wish other people see you.

None of us can stand to be lumped in a group that is not our choosing, especially a negative one. The late Bishop Fulton Sheen explained why you don't want to place labels on children. He tells a true story how he was sitting in a posh New York restaurant when he noticed a boy in a dirty T-shirt. The boy was occupied with swinging on the long plush drapes that lined the entrance into the restaurant. The maitre'd, noticing this, chased the little boy out of the restaurant and told him to never come back. The Bishop followed the distraught boy outside and asked him what his name was. Once the boy told the Bishop his name, the Bishop said it was a beautiful Irish name.

"You should be in Catholic school," the Bishop replied. The boy responded, "I go to public school. I used to go to Catholic school but I got kicked out." The Bishop assured the boy that he would get him back in, despite the fact that the boy's mother had tried several times to get him reinstated.

The next day, the Bishop went down to that school and met with the principle and the Mother Superior. He inquired why they kicked the young man out. The principle and the Mother Superior reiterated what the boy said. "He cannot come back here; his attitude is not accepted here." Hearing this, Bishop Sheen said, "Let me tell you a story about three boys who were kicked out of religious schools. The first boy was kicked out because he drew pictures while the class was going on. The second because he got in a series of skirmishes with other children, and the last because he had subversive pamphlets under his mattress."

The Bishop said, "Now no one knows who the valedictorian of any of their classes was but I'm sure that you are familiar with the three boys. The first was Hitler; the second was Stalin, and the last, Mussolini." The principle and the Mother Superior were shocked and let the boy back in school. The Bishop finished his story by telling us that the boy who was let back in school is now a missionary in Alaska. Surely what we look for in children or adults is what we will find. In Ephesians 6:4 it instructs parents, *"Fathers, do not irritate and provoke your children to anger (do not exasperate them to resentment), but rear them (tenderly) in the training and discipline and the counsel and admonition of the Lord."*

When to Punish and When to Spank

"We discipline
our children for the very
same behaviors we excuse
ourselves of on a
daily basis."

— Charles Rivers

As a Christian family you will live amongst a swirling barrage of opinions on the subject of discipline and your children. But remember if you can stick to the Creator's principles for discipline you can never go wrong with your little ones and yourself. Many people who were raised either the wrong way or in an abusive situation become either paralyzed to stop their children or paralyze their children by stopping everything they do.

Throughout the entire bible you will notice that God admonishes and praises in equal measure. His discipline was for those out of his will or those living out of the principles of love. His praises were for those operating in the laws of love. Only death and destruction came from hate while life and relationship building came from love. God's will is effectively keeping us in balance, protecting our very lives.

I sat with a father who still threatened his oldest son at age fifteen with whooping him. He had three other sons of younger ages that he screamed at to get them to do right. This father believed himself to be firmly in control of his children. But when you have to scream and carry on with strong discipline three years before your child goes into the world, you're the only person who lacks control. I made clear to the father that a whooping simply for the sake of discipline yields only immediate compliance.

If you spank a child who has not done his homework on a daily basis and is failing in school, you may see short term improvement. But soon enough, over time, those grades will drop off again until you have to lean on the spankings to maintain that grade point average. Another reason whooping alone doesn't work is because by itself it does not yield any lesson beyond getting whooped. Case in point, your child gets in a fight with a bigger child at school.

The older child is able to whoop your child in the playground conflict. Where is the lesson learned? The similarity to the whooping we gave is present. So when you spank your child and you only notice a pattern of immediate compliance, then change your approach. Raising little ones like this will turn them into adults who tell lies. As parents we have many occasions that are presented for giving our children lifelong lessons.

Tell your children the right thing to do even when you don't think they are listening. Even during the times that they appear to be staring into space. Their rebellious brains are absorbing those critical messages better than their little butts ever will a whooping on these occasions. If you don't believe me and you are now a parent yourself, look back at your own history. Think on the occasions where your grandparents or parents tried to impart lifelong messages in your brain before or after you did something wrong.

Now fast forward to today and see if you can recall most if not all of what they were trying to impart upon your life. Look at how those warnings and instructions prevented you from great harm. Look at how they helped to shape the career path you chose. You may have stared into space back then or murmured under your breath in secret, as all young people will do, but the message did stick. I have spoken to adults who have lost their parents at an old age and they still can recant messages that were imparted to them from fifty years ago.

So if you must spank your child, use these guidelines. Spank the child when you are first not in a state of offense or irritated. Occasions for being offended present themselves after a long day's work, or from behavior that is naturally childlike in nature. Our child must have done something worthy of it and you have to be in the right frame of mind to carry it out without making it personal. Remembering that you are not spanking your children but sending down a legacy of discipline to generations to follow through this one child.

Child Honesty Verses the Shameful Factor

All children start out primarily honest, as sent by God from above. Although they do learn how to manipulate to get what they want, the true sense of lying does not manifest until they get in trouble for the first time. No matter if you are an infant or an elderly person, all humans have a tendency to lie when they are not proud of something they have done. Children learn to be creative at lying to avoid spankings or punishment.

Look at every situation in the bible where God was about to bring discipline on someone for an offense. What did each person that knew discipline was coming in advance do? They either lied or made up an excuse to cover their transgression. So if you pick up a pattern of lies in your little one you may need to change your form of discipline. This is so that you don't teach them to lie more than you teach them to obey what is right. Finally your children will be fine with discipline if you only take just as much time to praise their positive behavior as you do to catch them doing something wrong.

It is our job as parents to put the best in our children God has to offer. We should never try to predict their future any more than we can predict our own. This is why we are instructed in Proverbs 22:6, *"Train up a child as you would have him go and when older he will never depart from it."*

This biblical passage recognizes that the child's free will as an adult can have him doing many things that will take him off of the narrow path to heaven and to the broad path to hell. But at the same time, it expects that they will return as long as the child within the adult has been rooted in love. Another bible passage that recognizes this is the Prodigal Son. In Luke 15:10 it states, *"Even so, I tell you, there is joy among and in the presence of angels of God over one (especially) wicked person who repents."* So even after doing your absolute best and having your child go astray, trust in God and pray for their faithful return as the Prodigal Son.

*"Conceive
in your minds eye
your child as being unique
and you will be a witness to
uniqueness."*

— Charles Rivers

Your little one was born for a time such as now, not for a time such as you grew up in. This is my advice to parents who want to prepare their children for the future. So when we affect warnings on their conscious, we have to ensure that they are not based solely upon the pains we went through, otherwise our children will be ill prepared for what life reveals to them.

Because your child is unique, the most difficult balancing act you will ever perform is to stop trying to heal your personal past through them. If you bring to bear the full weight of your pains or pleasures upon your children's individual existence, they will spend the rest of their adult life trying to shake it off. Trust me; I have sat in on too many sessions where the biggest concern of the adult is how they can start living their dreams instead of their parent's nightmare. It is not incumbent upon any of us to relive our parent's upbringing, especially if it was bad. God the Father presents this same logic throughout the bible. Did you know that

God never sent anyone through the same experience twice?

Some parents, molested in their youth, come to assume that children will be done the same unless we watch and restrict them harshly. Some adults faced poverty as children and fight for money at all costs. Others had too much money as children and they can recall no love to show that was equivalent to the value of that money. As adults these parents smother their children so they won't feel without love as they once did for the sake of money. But dealing with your little one this way is the same as discipline. Ensure that your advice or guidance is about the child and not about you.

Parents are more than providers to children; we are teachers to them. In fact, the longest school term anyone ever attended was not public or private but our home schooling. That's right: eighteen years of your life was spent in the classroom of your parents.

The classes we attended were familiar subjects like accounting, human relations and psychology to name a few. Sometimes, just like the real schools we attended, we weren't too fond of the teachers. Some teacher's behavior served little more than to push us in the opposite direction of our full potential. But just as with real schools, the teachers (parents) who see the best in us — even though we served up the worst — helped to shape and mold us for the future.

Living Within the Double Standard

It amazes me how we fight to keep our little ones out of all of the worst and most violent public schools and communities in our town but we create those same environments in our sanctified homes. Once our children are at the age to be liberated from our home schooling they will do everything in their power to live as secular a life as possible, publicly and privately. The most adults who run away from God and religion are the children who grew up in the homes of the religious parents.

Show Your Children God in Person

The character Saint Nicholas or Santa Clause has always been readily identifiable by children. He is well known for bringing children fun, magic and love during Christmas. He has only wanted the best for them and the best out of them. This is what it means to present God's love to the world. Let your children be able to easily identify you as the love that God expects them to one day live within, and you don't have to put on a red suit to do that. The two spiritual women I credit in my life who brought me to God did so by their actions in life and to life.

The first was my mother: she sparked the flame of God's love and understanding in my life. The other was a friend that I would not meet until I was much older in life. She reignited what my mother had begun in me many decades earlier. They could never have inspired me to believe by merely professing so with their mouths. God instructs us, as parents, to bring our children to him. We are judged by God if we miss the mark on this attempt. Jesus instructed his disciples who were trying to shoo children away in Matthew 19:14 to "*suffer the little children and let them come unto me, for such is the kingdom of heaven made up of.*"

If we as Christian couples take our children to church weekly and profess God with our mouths while arguing with our spouses at home, what must we expect from our children? We remain not much different than the secular crowd we forbid our children from hanging around. We simultaneously block them from God by our actions. You can't convince a child to take on a double standard if you disguise it as love. Hatred should not be accepted in our Christian homes or outside of it. When we dislike people who are indifferent to us, we stoop to their level of anger and indifference.

But when we choose to love those who hate us instead, we raise our standards to God's and reflect the true meaning of being a follower of Christ. Have you noticed that when people behave meanly towards you a surge occurs in your body that can change the smile on your face to a grimace? A similar behavior takes over parents when their children frustrate them — if they are in the wrong frame of mind.

The Teacher Must Learn From the Pupil in Order to be Effective

Each child is as individual as the home they are born into — with maybe one exception. Children bring light to where the glow of youth in the parents may have faded. We have much to teach our little ones by the age of eighteen, but have much more to learn from them by age five. Your child will reveal to you, through their nature, the humanity you lost in the process of becoming an adult. By the time the average couple decides to have children, they would have set their home up nicely where it is comfortable for adults. Parents will subsequently prepare a room wonderfully for a baby prior to its arrival.

But babies have no concept of boundaries between rooms or limits of other people's personal property. A toddler will throw up half a bottle of milk on your new expensive furniture along with your new clothing. That expensive crystal you bought prior to children becomes an attractive toy in their eyes, so you better place it up high if you want to keep it.

A toddler giggles for no reason other than simply because they enjoy the moment they are in, but take that same person as an adult and they will need the stimulus of alcohol, drugs or the like to loosen up and find a smile. Little ones are not like this any more than you were as a toddler. As a child you did not need drugs, legal or otherwise, to bring you up or down. You did not need caffeine to make it through the work day. Nor did you need alcohol to help you forget the week come Friday's celebration.

In the bible, it is written in 1 Corinthians 13:11 that, *"When I was a child I spoke as a child, I reasoned as a child but now that I am an adult I put away childish things."* But what that passage does not say is that I put away my humanity in order to become an adult. I believe that lost humanity, love for all, and compassion are the only things that separate us from children. But Jesus said unless we become as children again (at heart) we will never see the kingdom of heaven. As adults we have a tendency to prematurely age the life out of our children's childhood as it was done to ours.

We go from admiring the newborn's birth to planning what college our child is going to and how he or she can compete effectively with their classmates. We falsely believe that they need to act seriously as early as infancy for the world to take them that way. It is the behavioral equivalent to *Invasion of the Body Snatchers.* This movie's premise was that alien invaders used pods to replicate each human that they came in contact with in order to take their place in the world. The only thing the aliens could not replicate was the person's individual humanity and ability to have natural fun.

So once the person was converted they appeared to be nothing more than a robot without feelings. It was the job of those who had already been converted to seek out and reveal those who had not been. I remember vividly, towards the end, a character telling another, "I went to sleep and it didn't hurt me. You should go to sleep." The only way to convert someone was in their sleep, so when they awoke they would not be the same. This is exactly what we do when we encourage our children to put their humanity to sleep to become the walking dead.

All Children Have Built-In Mercury-Driven Temperaments

"Children will
let you know when
you have concentrated on
yourself long enough."

— Charles Rivers

If your children cannot get your positive attention, they will ultimately settle for your negative attention. If you cannot give them the time of day for their concerns, they will act out to bring your attention upon them. You see, children are the regulators or thermometers of every marriage. When a husband and wife go at one another, arguing and not getting along, it affects the children. No indifference in the home is just between the parents—it affects the home as a whole. If you have a school-aged child during home conflicts you will be witness to their grades dropping and their homework going undone.

Shortly thereafter you will begin to receive notes and telephone calls from their teacher concerning their work performance and attitude. The teacher will call mainly to prevent your child from failing; she will not be aware of your personal problems. But usually intervention from outside sources is enough to break the concentration between two warring adults, so as husband and wife we cease our strife and turn our attention towards our child to prevent them from failing. Over time, sure enough, the child's grades begin to climb and school behavior improves.

A great thing has just occurred courtesy of the Creator of the universe. God the Father placed a relationship regulator in children that they don't even know they possess. That is why children are successful at getting you to turn your attention and anger off of each other and back towards pressing needs. Additionally, the child has shown you that as a team there is nothing that you cannot do if you use your positive mind as well as you use the negative.

Have you noticed spikes or drops in your children's grades? If so find out where your relationship was at least ten days prior to that event. If you can bring your behavior in line with Agape love you can not only regulate your child's achievement but you can have all of the love you have ever dreamed of in a Christian family.

Children Are Like Little Camcorders

Children, since birth, are like tape recorders with a human body. They watch everything we do and they listen to everything we say. During their childhood the record button is stuck in the on position. But once they reach adult life they hit the playback button in their own personal lives. What is played back is what we allowed them to record of our behaviors, positively or negatively.

Now here is where things tend to get very difficult. If from your experience with them they cannot face life, they will hit the pause button and remain in place for as long as it takes them to go forward in the play mode. Unproductive years at a time will fly by in this mode. Pause in the lives of humans is usually a time for personal reflection on the past. It is equivalent to staring into a mirror or a calm pond. What happens when we stare at our image for a long time? The backdrop tends to fade away. People around us become invisible and so does what really is important in life. We must pull back from the stare to allow the rest of life to come in.

Once most people have taught themselves to get beyond the pause, they will hit fast forward in an attempt to catch up to their life. Most people who find the fast forward button have learned to do so mainly because of forgiveness for their past. They have finally come to understand what role their parents played and that their parents did not mean to harm them. If a person hits a brick wall with forgiveness they will hit the rewind button to go back and try to understand what happened. If what they recorded was beautiful, they can use it to enhance the present. If not, then God, psychiatry and self help books will be leaned upon to help them hit the stop button on self condemnation for something they had no control over. What most people need in that situation is to press eject to reject a non-Christian upbringing.

Teaching Your Children the Values of Love

*"You will never
know what you might
have received if you are not
willing to give up what
you already have."*

— *Robert H. Schuller*

Each milestone we attain as a couple draws our family closer together, closer to God. Each milestone you achieve independent of one another's advice shows proof of your unwillingness to cleave. Along the way, through your entire relationship, you will come upon pressures when you refuse to bend to change what will help the relationship get over your old ways that ruin relationships. It is twice as important to our children as is to us to witness our peaceful agreements as we seek to merge our different personalities.

The secret ingredient to merging two different backgrounds is to let them go. As a couple you are building a new home together, as I said before, and not rebuilding your childhood home. As humans we see change as loss but to be successful in any long term relationship you will have to see change as gain. The lesson your child will take away from your love interactions is that selfishness ends when you enter into a loving relationship.

Once you join with someone else in marriage you are not actually entering an Eros relationship but an Agape love that slowly manifests itself far beyond the flash-in-the-pan sexual love affair. Expect to lose a lot of self on the way to finding yourselves as a couple. Prepare to gain more than you would have if you were trying to hold on to what you lost. If one is to win at love, he or she must first be willing to lose at it well.

*"God is love,
and he who dwells and
continues in love dwells and
continues in God, and God
dwells and continues
in him."*

— *1 John 4:16*